Seeds of Inspiration

Also by Dorothy Maclean

The Living Silence

Wisdoms

To Hear the Angels Sing

The Soul of Canada

To Honor the Earth

Choices of Love

Seeds of Inspiration

Deva Flower Messages

Dorothy Maclean

The Lorian Association
PO Box 1368
Issaquah, WA 98027
www.lorian.org

Seeds of Inspiration

Cover art and design and interior illustrations
by Deva Berg

Edited by Freya Secrest and Susan Sherman

Published by The Lorian Association
PO Box 1368
Issaquah, WA 98027

ISBN 0-936878-08-8

Maclean, Dorothy
Seeds of Inspiration / Dorothy Maclean

Library of Congress Control Number: 2004100732

First Edition: March 2004

Printed in the United States of America

0 9 8 7 6 5 4 3 2 1

www.lorian.org

This book is dedicated to the fellowship between
God, humans and nature

Acknowledgements

Most of these flower messages are being published here for the first time. For those being reprinted I want to express my appreciation to Lindisfarne Books, the publishers of *To Hear the Angels Sing* and *Choices of Love,* and to all the others who have helped bring my messages into public view.

Deep thanks to Freya Secrest and Jeremy Berg for their suggestion to create this unique book focusing on flower messages and all their help to make it a reality. Also many thanks to Lynn Barton for researching the Latin names of the plants.

I

Contents

Flower Name   **Page Number**

Alkanet - *Anchusa officinalis* 48
Alyssum - *Alyssum saxatile* 6
Apple Blossom - *Malus x domestica* 21
Aster - 1967 - *Callistephus chinensis* 74
Aster - 1971 - *Callistephus chinensis* 75
Aubrietia - *Aubrietia deltoidea* 22
Azalea - *Rhododendron* 14
Bearded Iris - *Iris hybrids* 44
Broom - *Sarothamnus scoparius* 49
Busy Lizzie - *Impatiens walleriana* 94
Canterbury Bell - *Campanula meduim* 37
Castor Oil Plant - *Ricinus communis* 80
Chamomile - *Chamaemelum nobile* 76
Christmas Rose - *Helleborus niger* 96
Clematis - 1967 - *Clematis montana* 23
Clematis - 1970 - *Clematis montana* 24
Clove Carnation - *Dianthus caryophyllus* 81
Coleus - *Coleus blumei* 93
Cornflower - *Centaurea cyanus* 60
Daffodil - 1969 - *Narcissus* 4
Daffodil - 1970 - *Narcissus* 5
Daffodil - 1971 - *Narcissus* 2
Dahlia - *Dahlia hybrids* 84
Dandelion - *Taraxacum officinale* 1
Elecampane - *Inuia helenium* 57
Foxglove - *Digitalis purpurea* 63
Garden Rose - *Rosa hybrids* 53
Gentian - *Gentiana sino-ornata* 86

Glory of the Snow - *Chionodoxa luciliae* 13
Gloxinia - *Sinningia speciosa* 95
Godetia - *Godetia grandiflora* 91
Gorse - *Ulex europaeus* 18
Honesty - *Lunaria annua* 87
Honeysuckle - *Lonicera periclymenum* 47
Hyssop - *Hyssopus officinalis* 52
Ice Plant - *Mesembryanthemum criniflorum* 58
Iris Reticulata - *Iris* 27
Lady's Mantle - *Alchemilla mollis* 38
Lavender - *Lavandula angustifolia* 43
Leopard's Bane - *Doronicum cordatum* 25
Lilac (California) - *Ceanothus* 39
Lilac - *Syringa vulgaris* 40
Lily - *Lilium auratum* 77
Lily of the Valley - *Convallaria majalis* 8
Love Lies Bleeding - *Amaranthus caudatus* 78
Lungwort - *Pulmonaria officinalis* 30
Lupin - 1967 - *Lupinus hybrids* 61
Lupin - 1968 - *Lupinus hybrids* 62
Marigold - *Calendula officinalis* 73
Mexican Hat - *Kalamchoe diagremontiana* 64
Mock Orange - *Philadelphus* 20
Nasturtium - *Tropaeolum majus* 42
Night-Scented Stock - *Matthiola bicornis* 51
Orange Lily - *Lilium* 50
Ornamental Cherry - *Prunus* 16
Pansy - *Viola x wittrockiana cultivars* 31
Passion Flower - *Passiflora caerulea* 9
Periwinkle - *Vinca major* 11
Petunia - *Petunia x hybrida* 41
Pieris - *Pieris formosa forrestii* 17
Polyanthus - *Primula, Polyanthus Group* 29
Primrose - *Primula vulgaris* 19
Rhododendron - *Rhododendron ponticum* 15
Rose of Jericho - *Selaginella lepidophylla* 94
Salvia or Clary - *Salvia sclarea* 54
Saxifrage - *Saxifraga x urbium* 7
Scilla - *Scilla siberica* 8
Sea Pink or Thrift - *Armeria maritima* 28
Snowdrop - *Galanthus nivalis* 15
St. John's Wort - *Hypericum perforatum* 85
Sunflower - *Helianthus annuus* 83
Sweet Cicely - *Myrrhis odorata* 10

Sweet Pea - *Lathurus odoratus* 66
Sweet William - *Dianthus barbatus* 68
Tansy - *Tamacetum vulgare* 79
Tibetan Blue Poppy - *Meconopsis baileyi* 69
Tree Mallow - *Lavatera arborea* 45
Viola - *Viola odorata* 92
Wallflower - *Erysimum cheiri* 33
Water Lily - *Nymphaea* 56
Wild Rose - *Rosa canina* 42
Wild Violet - *Viola canina* 32
Wisteria - *Wisteria sinensis* 65
Yarrow - *Achillea millefolium* 67

VI

Introduction

Love is a bridge between all the kingdoms of nature

This book contains some of the communications with the intelligent essence of various flowers and herbs that I received from 1963 to 1973 while living at Findhorn, Scotland. Before these communications began, I had ten years of training and experience in connecting to the God within, which became the core of my life, and which also led to the experiment in conscious cooperation between humans and the nature kingdoms that evolved in the Findhorn garden.

Recognizing that there is an intelligence in nature that goes beyond our concept of the survival of the fittest and ecological diversity is not yet commonplace in our western culture. It requires a change in perspective that, for me, began in 1948 when I was greatly tested in my aim to lead a loving life. My determination—to me a sacrifice of what I loved most— led to an experience which changed me completely. I had an inner knowing that God was within and that I was part of a vast loving universe. So powerful was this moment that friends who saw me the next day wondered what had happened to me, as I was so different that even my voice had changed. The experience gave me the inner strength to act on my aim to be truly loving. Living alone after that, at quiet moments a thought kept coming to me to "Stop, listen and write." Although I first ignored it, eventually I followed that inner directive and wrote down wonderfully inspirational insights, finding my own words to translate the meaning of my experiences.

For ten years after that I kept a discipline of doing this several times a day. I, and others who were following a similar practice, listened to, acted on and tested these intuitions, until they became the basis of our lives and led us into helpful experiences. In 1962, when we settled at the Findhorn Bay Caravan Park and were attempting to grow vegetables in sand, I was told from within that I had a job to communicate with nature, and that everything in nature, even planets, clouds, and vegetables, had an intelligence. I was to attune to and harmonize with the essence of this intelligence. At first this seemed too silly an idea to be true, but eventually I did make contact with the essence of the vegetables that we were growing. I found I was communicating with formless energy fields, not the spirit of a single plant but the soul level of the species. I had no word for what I was contacting—"angel" was close but brought to mind harps and wings. As the Sanskrit word "deva," meaning "shining one" seemed closer, I used it.

These messages received from the intelligence of various flowers and herbs focus on the theme of the oneness of all life. In my contact, I generally did not ask questions. I just contacted the soul essence of the particular plant and let it communicate what it wished. All hoped that we humans would develop our inner knowing and contact them. To them it is necessary for the future of the planet that we recognize and cooperate with the invisible components of life on Earth, for only then can we change our ways and work with them for the health of the world as a whole.

Their perspective opened and enlarged my own. For example, the following passage from the Apple Deva talks about how creation occurs from their point of view:

You feel drawn to us by the clustered blossom and the promise of fruit to come. That from a fragile, scarcely colored and short-lived bloom a sturdy apple appears is but one of God's miracles enacted many times over for all to observe. If you could see more of how this is brought about by the chain of life, wonder would lift you high.

As from the seed a tree grows, so from the seed idea a pattern of force issues forth from the Center, passed on by silent ranks of angels, silent and still because the idea is still too unformed and unfixed to endure any but the most exacting care. Down and out it comes, growing in strength and size, becoming brighter in pattern, until eventually it scintillates and sounds, still in the care of the outmost great angels. Its force field is steady and brilliant.

Then the pattern is passed to the makers of form, the elements, who come up and give of themselves and clothe that pattern. Remember that this is a process, that the pattern is everywhere apparent in the ethers held by the angels and made manifest beyond time by the energy of the elements through the ministrations of the elementals at the appropriate opportunity. It then appears in time and place, eventually in the beauty of the blossom and the succulence of the fruit.

This is the Word made flesh. This is all creation, held in balance by great layers of life of which your conscious mind is unaware. A miracle? You need a greater word, you need to go beyond words.

The fruits of the earth are produced through the unsung and dedicated service of these many forms of life - and we hope that the gardeners at your end of the line are as happy in their work! You, humans, have the fruits, although you do little of the work. So it is. May your praise be greater than ours, which never ceases.

Always I found joy at the core of the nature presences. They talk of that and of many things: of their constant awareness and praise for what I call the love of God, their awareness of our true nature, their desire for cooperation with us, their view of how we can best develop ourselves and find a light-heartedness and sense of fun similar to theirs, and on and on. The wonderful qualities which I found in them, different in each plant, are qualities which we humans also contain. By becoming at one with them in this inner way, we strengthen those qualities within ourselves and emerge strengthened in what we are.

The messages in this book are from two different sources. The Preface includes messages from my inner divinity that helped me develop my early understandings of the devic realm. They point out that it is not necessary to have contact through words—appreciation, gratitude and love create the links. The flower messages themselves follow, divided into seasonal categories for easy access: Spring, Summer, Autumn and Winter, the latter basically consisting of pot-plant contacts.

The drawings we hope will provide yet another doorway into the essence underlying the beauty of plants.

Dorothy Maclean
August 2003

X

Preface

In this Preface I am sharing various communications that I received from my inner divinity introducing me to my work with the devic world. I had to be given help, instructions, and information about the devas — and my own sense of limitation—to make it easier for me to stretch into their dimensions. I hope that my messages, which represent my understanding at the time, will also help you, the reader, to more easily move into these invisible worlds.

Inner Guidance

Yes, you are to co-operate in the garden. Begin this by thinking about the nature spirits, the higher nature spirits who overlight, and by tuning into them. That will be so unusual as to draw their interest here. They will be overjoyed to help and to find some members of the human race eager for that help. This is the first step. The smaller, individual nature spirits are under their jurisdiction.

By the higher nature spirits, I do not mean just the ones that geographically overlight the area, but the spirits of the different physical forms, such as the spirits of clouds, of rain, and of the separate vegetables. In the new world, their realms will be quite open to humans – or I should say, humans will be open to them – and when rain is needed, for example, it will be brought about. It is even possible with you now, if your faith were great enough to have no sense of limitation. Now just be open and seek into the glorious realms of nature with sympathy and understanding, knowing these beings are of the Light, willing to help but suspicious of humans and on the lookout for the false, the snags. Keep with Me and they will find none, and you will all build towards the New.

9 May 1963

There is no such thing as dead matter; everything is living and everything has a place in My one life. That life force is more than what you call magnetism. It is an influence unconsciously wielded on the

XI

higher levels. You are simply surrounded by life; you are a life force moving among other life forces. As you recognize this and open up to them, you draw near to them, become more and more one with them, and work with them in My purposes. You are drawing away from a self-centered, little world and are entering the vast, new worlds where life is one because it all works together for My good.

29 May 1963

Yes, listen to the sounds of nature whenever you have the chance. They are true sounds, coming from Me within each, and can lead you into My world. When you are close to Me and listening, you are tuning yourself into worlds of growth and forces which are always present and have a tremendous effect on humans unconsciously. When you are conscious of them, they open up and reveal how you are all linked. Do not worry if you seem to get no specific message from these worlds. As you tune into them, your link with them grows and may bear fruit in a slightly different direction. Keep positive and tune in.

16 July 1963

You are pioneering in the true attitude to nature, to the one life. For this attitude it behooves you to think of everything in terms of life force – not merely an impersonal force like electricity, but as a manifestation of some being. Not only that, for the beings behind the various manifestations are conscious representatives of Me. They can teach you and help you, though what you see of them outwardly may be a lowly bee, a leaf, or a stone. Behind all is a great chain of life, leading to Me. Humans on Earth have been given dominion over all these on Earth, but only as you, too, fit into the great chain of life.

It is for you to stretch out and learn how to fit in, to use all of the gifts that I have given humankind for the advancement of all life according to My purposes. You are all elastic enough, if you will, to touch and enter My many realms, and it is up to you to do so with Me. Extend your own nature. Be open and feel out, in the fullness of the love I give you, and help to make My one life become reality on all levels.

2 October 1963

XII

My child, I talk of the one world and the interrelation between all life, but there has to be effort to reach into this new conception. It is new, newer than you think. It is not the same as the ties of the old world which humans form through life. These ties of the personality you take for granted, but they have to be broken down before the delicate new ties are felt. The old ties are built up on the conception of each of you as being a separate entity related to other entities. The new ties are built on the conception of you being part of the greater with no separate life. There is a clear distinction between these two.

The best way for you at the moment to develop real relationships is to stretch into My one world as you sense it. For instance, both your physical body and your more subtle bodies are fed by, and composed of, the life force developed by the devas. You are, therefore, part of them and they are part of you. You could not exist in your present form without them They realize this, but you are only beginning to do so. The more you stretch into their being, the closer you come to the basic forces used for your life. All this, of course, under Me. This is simply the way I fashion life.

All this with and without feeling: with, in the sense that you are feeling more into the unity which life is; without, in the sense that there is no false sentiment in the way life is used for life, and always with knowledge and gratitude. Call it an extension of feeling. Relationships in the old were rather like two dead ends being connected, for, once established, they were inclined to stay static and not grow. In the new, each relationship is living, changing, and new. This in itself takes effort. Nothing can be taken for granted. Always, there has to be an opening out and reaching for further horizons. A concrete example of this is the fact that a deva you know will make a quite different impression the next time you contact it, so be not surprised or puzzled. Know that life is moving. Keep very open to all this under My guidance, and let Me lead in this very wonderful but different new world.

26 October 1963

Devas

Do you know that the very thought of mankind about a plant makes contact with the deva world? It is not a great contact and it is not lasting but, nevertheless, humans in their thought world have crossed into our world. As we are there, if you are sensitive or in line with the inner, your thoughts can be and are influenced by us.

When we talk about one world, it is reality, not idle talk. You, humanity, may know nothing whatsoever about this, but that does not make it any less true or unreal. If you realized just how much your thoughts impinged on others and on other worlds, you might be more careful, for your thoughts are indeed far-reaching. Every thought has an influence, for it is life-moving, and how seldom it moves in a constructive direction! Blessed are the pure in thought - and powerful too!

21 December 1963

The nature spirits and the spirits of the elements do not have a birth, lifespan, and death, as humans do. They simply arise to meet a need, to fulfill a function, to undertake a purpose. Take the wind, for example, or a fire. When the life forces that comprise these elements are strong enough and there is wind or fire, the spirits of the wind or the fire are there, present, born in that instant, to vanish from whence they came in the next instant. The spirits of the plants come out of the great store of life force for a purpose and return to it, when their purpose is achieved.

This makes our world sound like a very work-a-day one – only in existence for a purpose. That is so, and yet, it is not so in the normal human meaning. Our work is our play, our forces are vividly channeled in the present, and we are forever in the present. Even, when we are not in manifestation, we are in the great stream of life force to some purpose. Our Creator and your Creator can quite easily, always, find a purpose for us, because life is meant to be enjoyed, to be lived. Now we go back from whence we came, leaving this thought with you.

2 January 1964

Just tune into nature until you feel the love flow. That is your arrow into the deva world. It does not matter if there is a message or not; it is the state which counts. It is always your state that the nature world responds to – not what you say, not what you do, but what you are. If you are depressed, you will not find harmony with us, but if you turn to us strongly enough, you will lose your depression. If your mind goes in circles, questioning, you will find no harmony with us, but if you stay long enough, you will find peace. The nature world is indeed the expression of perfection on Earth in matter. When this perfection is also found in humans (which is when you find yourself in a state of harmony with all) then, indeed, life flourishes and then, you will find instant co-operation with us. It all depends on your being what you are – a God-spark functioning in matter consciously. Be joyful. Lift yourselves. Be at one with us. We welcome you more than you know, and will continue to. Thank you.

1 May 1972

Spring

Dandelion

I am greatly honored to come into the garden by the front door! It does make a difference in the bond between us and humanity when we come at your desire instead of in spite of yourselves, for with your aid the plant can expand and do of its best. Let us show what we can do in cooperation. Nevertheless, I hope to be greeting you from odd corners.

Daffodil - 1971

Everywhere we proclaim the triumphant message of re-birth, of a new season. The air vibrates with this theme. You breathe it in with every breath, and, although your general consciousness may be elsewhere, every atom of your body responds. What a lot you miss as you go around with your focus on the little interests that cut you off from the vitality of the life around you, from the resurgence of life expressed outwardly in the fresh greenery of the plants, and inwardly in a fresh response to cosmic energy!

Life is new. The newness is different in each season. You are different from what you were a year ago. All life is different and therefore each spring is distinct, to be specifically aware of, to be reached into.

Our world tunes into the outpouring of energy naturally, because we are the wielders of that energy. It simply comes to us from all sides in the rhythm which is universal law, the farthest stars reflecting oneness with the tiniest substance of earth as we swing into spring. Cosmic Beings greet us as this small planet turns to its place of rebirth. Their intelligence knows this is our time of resurgent life, for all fits in. All is one, and all energies flow, exchange and compliment each other in the great related movement which is universal life. Each planet at its appointed time - if it deals with time and place - responds to and gives from itself a new outburst of life, and this is for you here and now.

All around you creation shows its part of the oneness of life, but what of many human minds? We see them caged and colorless, attached to non-essentials or even militant against the progression of life. What a marvel it would be if they were everywhere aiding the great energy release of the time, playing their part in fullest expression! What extra joy there will be in spring when human minds join in!

Our world of energy is offering life new opportunities to be itself. From every daffodil we trumpet a call of new beginnings, of perfection, purity and color, renaissance. Everywhere is the same message, particularly for humans. Respond, we say. All life is yours, the world and all therein, the kingdoms of love and the kingdoms of light and the children thereof. Join us in the oneness of life, and with us give eternal thanks to the One.

Daffodil - 1969

Yes, we would speak. We are so active here that we would brush upon your imagination and remind you that we are alive, very much alive. We love the rain, the ground, your love, the light, the warmth, all of God's creation which comes together so intensely at this time and causes the flowers to vibrate and be. We would sing of the spring that comes to earth. We would have it ripple through the land and wave golden in the air. We would have all read the message of joy that its Creator made it for.

Flowers talk in many tongues: in color, scent, texture. Today we would add a message in your language to try to convey something of the exultant Love of God which would clothe the universes with beauty and make that beauty sing and shine and smell and feel, giving life to the vehicles with which to appreciate all this and yet still remaining more than it, pure and joyful, remote yet ever present.

Oh, we would sing of life, but we cannot give you any idea of its power. You see the little details of it. You feel an indescribable essence. But do you know that it is all one, one exploding mightiness held together with ineffable strands of knowing Love spread through the millennia? There are no words there. There is this Life, this infinite perfection which will not move but to greater joy and perfection. What is time or space, life or death, galaxies or specks of dust, but material with which to create a greater perfection?

When you fall short of our ideal, which humans do, come and look at one of our flowers and raise yourself into the immensities of God's perfection. Then go on, worshipful and rejoicing, your soul lifted in praise with us to the One who is all in all.

Daffodil - 1970

Our activity here is beginning to fizzle out but it is still intense enough to vibrate predominantly in the garden. Wherever you turn at this particular time of gladness, there we are to greet the eye and the inner senses. A special time it is, when after the quietude of winter we and others show the freshness and beauty which is part of God's scheme for the earth, the promise of eternal life perfectly expressed. Surely the spring flowers are the symbol of the renewal of life. We feel this a privilege and joy. Yet one cannot talk of privilege in our realm, where life is simply a fluidic state, a changing, happy flow. Perhaps we express this best in spring when on every side plants and flowers are suddenly and magically blossoming, and each little note of color calls out clearly until a carpet of color appears. What was lifeless is alive. What was drab is aglow. Where there was nothingness is pattern. Miraculously on all levels you have something to respond to. The very air is full of sound and movement, for spring has come and everywhere life is tingling. How we relish the excitement of it!

You wonder if after this period we are quiescent until next spring. We are much more plastic and maneuverable than you. Whereas our consciousness of daffodils is quite distinct, it is also part of the whole, in a sense like ocean spray separating and then falling back into the whole. Humans are forever separating and keeping to classification; our separation is a movement of the whole. Of course each bulb is distinct and separate, but the life force in it is of the One, from and returning to the One, and that is our all. We devas are ever aware of this, of the One, of the life that upholds us. Hence the joy which always comes with us. Life is that One, and in the springtime we express it for all to see.

Alyssum

Become small and enter into our exuberance, which is large enough to enfold you. To you, it feels rather like the generous love of a large-hearted person and, indeed, there is a connection, for the special characteristics of a plant may be akin to those of a human, although on another order. We blaze forth to the world at large; some flowers and some humans have a delicate, single bloom attracting the attention of few.

So we say (and it seems to be necessary to say this) that you should not all try to be in the foreground as we are, very obvious in our own way and unlikely to be overlooked. You should not all try for the overflowing heart which you may greatly admire, but you should seek deep, deep for your own note. Your special characteristics may be like those of the wild violet, hidden among other species and very quiet, but just as perfect as the more grandiose plants. We see in human strivings attempts to be like this or that show flower. You attempt to mold yourselves to the pattern of someone you admire, of someone who has touched your heart, or of someone who is popular, when, all the time, the perfection which is yours and yours alone is encased within, unable to be.

God is within each one of you. Think of that! Let that truth seep into you. Let it be the central force, which it is. With your minds you think this or that, hovering to express this and that, when the absolute perfection of you – which has nothing to do with anyone else – is there waiting. Of course, the teachings of the enlightened ones can help, but the way lies within, where the seed of perfection is. Each one of us is truly aligned to that pattern within. Though you cannot but admire the various beauties of the flowers, each one of you has an even greater beauty.

We would urge you, with each glowing, yellow floret in our clumps of color, to be like us in your ardent expression of God's pattern for you, and to be quite unlike us, to be yourself, which is even better and closer to God.

Saxifrage

We quietly radiate to you, and it is as if you must stop and listen to us. Our flowers are fine and delicate, held firmly in place, and silently give forth their message. Our succulent leaves you find unattractive, which somehow makes the flowers all the more beautiful. Each plant has its appeal, testifying to the infinite variety and exquisite coloring of nature.

Come more deeply to us and feel the steady raying-forth. What strength and purity a small plant can convey! It is a world of its own, a sacred world, because the pattern is clear and clean and nothing interferes with it. Once established, a plant holds its own and is. Left to itself, nothing can deter it from its firm destiny. It knows where it is going; it shines forth without deviation; it fulfils its purpose.

Yes, if only mankind were to do likewise! If you knew your purpose, if you went towards it in all ways, steady in the pattern which is individually yours and following it regardless, you would be transformed. You too would radiate calmness and beauty. Do you do this even for a moment? What are the moments when you do? You cannot answer that because such moments are those when "you" are forgotten and your God pattern shines out. We represent one tiny aspect of the pattern of a human, but because we follow it as a harmony in the whole, the representation is perfect. You have many more facets, but you, all of you, cloud them with the separated self. In comparison, the perfection of a little flower pales all your gifts.

We know, when you more truly represent your Creator, your perfection will be glorious, and we shall rejoice and continue to radiate quietly wherever we are. Our serene happiness – and more – will be yours. Meantime, we continue to be ourselves, while you learn and move towards that fulfillment. It is one life, wonderfully expressed. We hope always to tell you that!

Lily of the Valley

We should love to bring our presence into your garden, for we draw so much good from humans as you respond to our sweet warmth. We link with you here and with our plants, over the face of the earth, in glad response to the great Giver of Life, whose plans are so perfect, and smile at the joyous work ahead of us.

Scilla

We felt the love and attention given to us in this garden from humans, and in our shy way have gloried in it, because the glory is given to God by you also. After all, the intensity of our blue is an intensity of adoration too. In little places we sound our note, and, as you know, in our world there are no barriers of space. As you pause before us and glorify our Maker in a silent wonder, all over the world, in the little places, the effect is felt by us.

You do not realize how powerful are human influences. All over the world we may be admired, or we may not even be seen. When you humans do link up in the One Life, as we do, and give the glory to the Divinity of Life, being in tune with all power, you can influence events more than thousands of others whose energy is unconsciously spent in all directions. It is important that this garden be a focal point in this way and all over the world. We know it, because we can feel it, feel the attuned life and blend with it. Thus we know that all is well; for as one man can save a city, so one garden can save a world. We know all this; you take the initiative and do not really know what you are doing.

We are always glad to pass on some of our awareness of life to you, as you come and tune in, and so we grow closer in understanding.

Passion Flower

Although my name has given me a special sanctity among humans and I am rather tall and towering, I am just as free and onward-moving as any of us. I come to you not only because you have marveled at the passion flowers, but because I would emphasize our Oneness. All that I am - in height, depth and breadth, in intricacy, wildness, beauty, pinpoint perfection, sweetness of purpose - is also what you are, is contained in you, is you.

When will you humans realize your dimensions and cease stalking the Earth as if you were form alone, molding other forms to suit yourselves? You are as vast, as free as we are, and more. You are mighty beings and you are pure, but you focus on mental unrealities and limit yourselves beyond belief. We can see what you are; you obviously see yourselves darkly. We would bring light into your thinking.

For a long time we have shared with you what we are, and you have rejoiced and been uplifted by these glimpses into our kingdom. Your heart and mind have expanded at the wonder of this corner of God's world. You have even known that, although seemingly impossible, all this is within you, but you have accepted the seemingly impossible aspect rather than the reality of what you are. We declare with passion that if you accept and act on your knowing, harmony would be everywhere, from your own warring natures to as far as imagination would take you. You, every one of you, would glide in freedom as we do, in rhythm with others, giving a helping hand to those still learning and reaching in themselves for greater dimensions of oneness. You would work in joy, sharing the presence of the Beloved. What fulfillment you have, what destiny! Yet you go round blindfold, chained, burdened, bowed, petty, mean. What nonsense! Look at any flower and know you are that and more. Look at any human and know you are that and more. Look to God and be that. We are all one, and it is your function to be so on all levels. We will keep reminding you, but you, you can bring joy to all worlds.

We are glad to have more than one plant in the garden now, and glad of any expansion in the contact between our worlds.

Here from source we shine our pattern, the particular aroma which is our contribution to the whole. It is very still, peaceful and immensely powerful, for from here we hold the threads which eventually form manifestation on earth.

We are taking you into this tremendous stillness to share with you more of our realms. Last time we manifested change, this time a living, dedicated stillness. Part of the consciousness of the angelic world is always rooted in this power. You too have your roots in this stillness, which is beyond words. But you are generally unaware of it, although you connect with it a little at times when you feel purpose or glimpse wholeness. Mystics talk of the still, small center. That has meaning for you, but this still center of ours is a vast, great stillness - yes, because our consciousness is not so individualized. We must have this great stillness so strongly in our make-up that nothing from outside is able to change the patterns we hold. Where there is great sensitivity - and there is here, close to source - it is essential that it be balanced by and rest on great strength, so that the Will of God within that strength be done on all levels. There is nothing but that Will. We hold our pattern of it in the stillness .

You see the difference from the little wills of men so often pitted against one another and so often petty. The devas share this gigantic stillness, and in fact so do you in your "higher" selves. We are not so different. All are part of the whole. We (we and you) are all shining beings. We all come from and return to the even greater Stillness, which is God.

That you could use a weed killer, knowing this, is unbelievable and tragic. Do not be upset at receiving this. We would bring home to you the reality of Oneness that you may act on it at all levels.

We devas pour our blessing down on the human race. We can do this because we are blessed and are close to the great Stillness. We never deviate from it, and we praise God in all creation.

Periwinkle

We would make contact, feeling the love that is there for us.

Flowers are great unifiers. All over the world, whatever language is spoken and whatever name we have, the human feeling for us can be the same. We link you all in the same positive transcendent wavelength. When you are consciously aware of this, connections are stronger. This may seem a nebulous fact at present, but as consciousness of the reality of oneness grows, the fact is continually brought to notice. It must be, and it is. The plant world has always whispered the fact. Now all worlds of nature shout it and are being heard.

From wherever we are, we proclaim our message of oneness and all the attributes of oneness. Beauty we proclaim in color, shape and scent, interdependence we proclaim, and perfection and the glory of God. Books we do not write; books are written about us. Life abundant we proclaim, in all its variations, and the wisdom of God through the ages. Inspiration we give to those who attune to us. We lift, we raise consciousness without words, and though words are being used in this contact, better still is the wordless communion we may have with any who stop for a moment and unite with us. We exalt activity in you and in ourselves, but communion of spirit on "higher" levels is part of co-creative life. We, and others like us, are always here to share our purity. We are part of one another in essence. Let us always be aware of that, and thank God for it.

Glory of the Snow

Although a small flower, we fill the room with our presence because at this time of blooming we are all that is, having expanded to the horizon. We acknowledge our oneness with all life but, being occupied in this matter of perfectly expressing the forces given to us, nothing else impinges. Are you not the same, completely absorbed when you are most truly yourself? If you are not, if you are half-hearted in what you do, then you divide your forces and fall short in achievement.

Each time you tune into the deva world you touch one aspect of us, generally aspects or qualities which have some relevance to you at the time or which we wish to stress. For instance, you have not come across the technicalities of the structure of leaf, root, or flower any more than you are aware of the technicalities of the function of your own body. These are part of our beings, but the wisdom of where consciousness is focused is a wonderful thing. We keep shouting of the joy of the deva world, or share its purity, or point you to the Source of all, because these are what are given us to say from the all-knowing One. So, while still filling all space with the pattern of a blue flower, we also pass to your receiving ear truths which apply to your world, truths which your consciousness has to contain. For you can choose now what you are conscious of. You do not have to remain in an unpleasant spot in your consciousness unless you choose to. You can find the good and the perfect where you are, and in love join with all worlds, even your own!

How we love to fulfill our task of bringing perfectly into form that which is unformed in your eyes! The energy used for this is channeled in exactitude, yet radiates through all dimensions, because love goes everywhere. Therefore we are one, and yet we are all. It is the same with all life. Now is the time for human consciousness to know this and act on it. The message comes from all life near and far, and will keep on coming until human consciousness has accepted and acted upon it. Then another aspect will be foremost.

In the passing, enjoy each one of us separately. Each plant, all of life, is an example of oneness individualized. Appreciate each. We all say it differently, but we all give the glory to the One.

Azalea

We come in, free and wild. Although much cultivated by humans, we retain an apartness that is our nature. We give beautiful blossoms seemingly from bare winter limbs, as if proving that with God all flower in their rightful time and season according to individual patterns.

You feel as though we are very attached to the conditions of our homeland although you do not know where that is. Yes, all of us are. Certain conditions brought us to perfection. We may thrive in other surrounds, but not with the facility we feel in our native land. That is again why wild flowers have a quality and fittingness not felt in a cultivated garden, and why the wild flowers of a country like Canada, for example, where there was no previous human cultivation, are outstanding in their uniqueness.

You ask if this deficiency can be overcome. We do not see how it can, completely. Such has not been our experience. On the other hand, perhaps the solution has not been tried on us. It might be that if the humans who transplanted us, so to speak, gave us enough love, this would overcome our homesickness and make up for the lack of the perfect conditions. Perhaps you would try this here, all of you, and let us report back to you later on.

This matter of home conditions is a very deep one in our kingdoms and of relative recent origin. Though you know that I, the Deva of the Azaleas, am everywhere at once, I am in my full beauty in my native land where the air I breathe, if I breathed, has a certain rarity. But we are most willing to go with the plan and learn. Already this contact with you has helped, because you are asking us and genuinely want to know. It is a refreshing change!

This experiment promises new things. We will do our part.

Snowdrop

I am glad that you have come to contact me, for although my forces here are tenuous, the contact is one that I am glad to renew. I am very much beloved in your country; it is good to feel that and to have it here, likewise. A tender regard from humans means much in our worlds.

Rhododendron

Vivid and somber, sunshine and rain, and over all a great love for being, a tenacity and exclusiveness, we settle in wherever we can, and get down to the business of being. We thank you for bringing us into the garden. We thank all who have allowed us roothold and life throughout the country, for we do like to settle.

Each species contributes to and changes the character of the land. Just as your human evolution is moving out of functioning as separated individuals or specialized groups, so is the plant world changing and the flora is becoming less specialized and more typical of the whole Earth.

Link with us whenever and wherever you see us. This is good for our relationship. Notice us and the way we grow. See us with new eyes. It will help you to imbibe our unique qualities. The philosophy and the plant life of a country are more related than you might think. Now that greater world unity is coming, let us not lose the essence of each unique contribution. Let us be friends.

Ornamental Cherry

We dance into the garden in our spring colors - why should we not be dressed in our best finery? We bless each of our plants, not stopping at them but including others in this season of joy. This is our expansive time, and we are firmly linked here. We are firm in many places, and cannot envisage it any other way in this spring when we beautify the Earth and call forth delight from all who see us. This is the time when the sun shines to bring life and the rain comes to hasten it, when the birds sing as never before. This is a time of general rejoicing. This is our time. We are in a jubilant mood. All cooperate with us, all are lifted out of the ordinary to what is ordinary in our world, the high joy of life abundant expressing itself now.

Yes, 'all' means humans. Human atmosphere is very predominant on Earth. Human thoughts and emotions are strongly present, influencing layers of life. Not often do you come into the layer I am talking from, which is a great pity, because you can do this. In reality this is more your home than the heavy lower levels that so many of you frequent. You are out of your depth in the depths where you live. You should be co-creators with us, also using the sparkle of life in your accomplishing. Your powers are equal to ours and greater - and what a strange mess you make with them! What a world this would be if you rode high, as high as we do, and all of creation were one in the joy of the Lord! How this old/young world would respond and shake off its shackles! We are in this world, you are in this world. Let us rejoice together and perfect it. Let us be gay and happy. This is the season, now.

Remember us, don't just file this message away. You are hearing a true voice, and every single human has within a voice like ours, uplifting and rejoicing. Listen and act. And thank you.

We would speak and be welcomed in. It is a joy to be in this experimental garden, and we settle in happily.

We would mention something of the forces that play through each plant. We are all different: the leaves are different, the flowers are differently shaped and colored, the way growth proceeds is different. We stand stationary, unlike you mobile humans who have a fairly standard pattern. Each of us is supremely planned to emit a certain aura, to have a certain influence, and to portray a certain idea of God. When we are at our best we stand as a perfect example of an idea, and all who momentarily stop and admire are helped. Any example of an idea of God, wonderfully expressed and constantly there, must uplift humans who aim for, but fall short of, perfection. Never mind the limitations of a plant; in its own sphere it is beauty itself, and clearly radiates out an untroubled uniqueness which is healing.

Pause when you see a plant in full bloom. Stop and forget to think, and just be aware of this symbol of the glory of God. For a second perhaps you may lose yourself and become wonder, and wondering move close to the purity of God. In this state you are non-resistant to the will of the whole, as is a plant, and perhaps will make a step to that original condition. Step or no step, you have been lifted. You are a more aware person; you have shared in a gift of life. The plant stands serene and radiant in its beauty, sharing with all who choose, and overflowing itself into its surround. What if the bloom is transient? Life moves on, and an unchanging bloom could become dull or be taken for granted. Our moments of splendor are part of the perfection of God's plan. Appreciate all things, and with us give full praise to God.

Gorse

We stand as guardians of the dunes, guardians of encroaching waste, with roots deep in the earth, with scent and color broadcast. We keep vigil on this plane, with prickles to keep out outsiders. Some plants have a higher function. We are on the lowest - and yet do we not reach to the highest in this our glory? We adorn the desert, we transmute this barrenness, we lift it to the heights and yet at the same time we stay spanning all levels, one of God's most useful creations. Normally we are transported by our golden glory. Today we show you another side of our nature, and still we keep the oneness which is the nature of all life. We keep it and shout it from every blaze of flower on every side.

The sun comes out and immediately we lighten and lift the contact. You feel now the ripples of golden light coursing out in continuous waves, feel it touch and transform the air, feel it run through your mind and heart and bring tears of gladness to your eyes. Feel the essential gorse-ness of us, which is God, God-ness. Always we have this message to spread if you stop, listen and hear. You seldom stop and listen, though you have heard us calling, calling over the moors straight to all open hearts. The strength of that call is almost overpowering. We are glad you answered it, for it is God the Highest calling. Make no division. Glory in God, glory particularly in us in season. The fact that we touch your heart so much binds our kingdoms together - and we as guardians and transformers should be one in our purposes, for there is a world to be saved.

We are torn and ground to dust as you machine us out of the way. We are untouched by this, but it is not right. We are as much part of Divine Life as you are, and while we must keep apart in our waste places, yet when we meet with you there should be communion and a sharing of intention. No part of creation should be taken for granted.

You wonder if you are merely writing down your own thoughts, if we would really speak in this vein. Why should we not? All is not sweetness and light in this world, and there is much that humans can learn from the plant kingdom, particularly from the intelligent beings responsible for this kingdom. Do not deny our voice. Do not expect it to be or say the same thing always.

Sense behind me the Landscape Angel, and higher and higher hosts in direct line of ascent to the Highest. They have much to do with this world, quite as much as humans. Yet as you use the results of their doing, how often do you acknowledge or consult or thank any of us? This becomes more and more urgent as more and more the Earth is despoiled. Yes, despoiled.

You know the joy and delight of our kingdom. We share it gladly with you and with everyone. But humans must recognize that we too are part of the One Life and that you cannot continue to only take from us and never give, or only give for your own selfish purposes. You must think in larger terms. You must think of the whole of the Earth, and not undermine it and give so little. You should be helping the mineral, vegetable and animal kingdoms, not using them. We know you know this. Nevertheless, let us repeat it, for it is important, and who knows who will listen. You are a listening ear and we have this to say, so we say it and hope that you may pass it on to those who will not listen directly.

Our realms have much of our consciousness to pass on. You look at the wonder and beauty of our blossoms, and marvel that limited plants could communicate in this way. You forget we are part of the One Life. We do our bit in bringing heaven down to earth, and we would have you do the same. There is much to be done. Join us in the one whole of all life.

Primrose

You have helped us spread ourselves and we are grateful. We like to greet the spring, in as many places as possible, whether or not we are admired. We are so glad to be able to be.

Mock Orange

We are here before you think of us. We are always with our plants. We are attached to each little charge because we love to see it grow, have the keenest delight in being part of its development out of nothing into a perfect example of the pattern we hold. Not one little pore is out of line. Out of the elements we carve and unite, and carve again a living example of one design of the Infinite Designer.

And what fun it is! Holding each little atom in its pattern is a joy. We see you humans going glumly about your designs, doing things without zest because "they have to be done," and we marvel that your sparkling life could be so filtered down and disguised. Life is abundant joy. Each little bite of a caterpillar into a leaf is done with more zest than we sometimes feel in you humans - and a caterpillar has not much consciousness. We would love to shake this sluggishness out of humans and have you see life as ever brighter, flowing, more creative, blooming, waxing and waning, eternal and one.

While talking to you I am also peacefully promoting growth in the plant. All over the world wherever I grow, I hold the wonderful designs for each plant to confirm. Maintaining life in countless places, I yet remain free, utterly and completely free, because I am the life of the One. How I rejoice to be alive! I soar to highest heaven, I become part of the heart of all. I am here, there and everywhere, without deviation holding my pattern of perfection. I bubble with life. I am life. I am One and I am many.

I have leapt lightly into your consciousness. I bow out, glad to have been with you, glad that you have appreciated what I have said, and still more glad to be back in our world of light. Think well of us, think of us with light.

Apple Blossom

Yes, we have been hoping for this inner contact with you. Why? Not merely because of friendliness, but because there is a need for the cultivated - shall we say, commercial - plants to contact humanity on truer levels than the usual. Our function is to produce and there is nothing we like better, whether it be blossom or fruit, but the spirit in which we are surrounded by humans is often out of truth and no thanks is given to the great Producer of all. Even the great Angels breathe out praise, and thus make room for the incoming breath. Also, this world is upset on the physical levels and beset by "freak" happenings and as the physical levels are the least enduring, it is good to build relationships on the more permanent levels.

We would take you gladly to our realms of truth and freedom, of that beauty you get a glimpse through our delicately colored blossom, but we would have you know that we are concerned with the character of the outer and physical. No, that has not always been our concern, for we have just gone along with the realms ordained for us. But there are changes which impinge on our consciousness, changes in the world recently which have not had a pattern of "good" for the devic life. You say this may be due to the raising of the world vibrations and therefore is good. Perhaps so, but we feel something will have to crack on the physical.

You do not understand why that lovely light buoyancy that comes with any of us is not present in this contact. It is there in the seed pattern. It is there and we are connected with it, but it is overlaid in our species with a heavy pall. You say that all is well, that God is guiding. That we can accept; that is what has been lacking. In that we find our freedom and we share it with you. We are beautiful, free and true, and would stay that way and produce in God's world. Thank you.

Aubrietia

With joy our particular contribution to the plant world obtains a toehold in the garden! You can feel what you translate as our jolliness, our always showing a shining face in our small way whatever happens.

There is a store of good-will with some of us for humanity. Some of us are quite tame! You will find this more in ones like me, in flowers. You did not find it with the vegetables which are even more cultivated by people than we are, because vegetables are grown to feed you and seldom get any appreciation. We are purely decorative and only get appreciation, and we don't have to provide fruits for your consumption. So we can be happily tame while many vegetables are unhappily tame. Yet they are more essential to you in many ways. Why do you not appreciate them as you do us? Yes, we are more colorful, but they have a beauty of their own which can be appreciated just as much as our vivid coloring.

It is easy to see the spark of the God-head in us. We do not cover it up as you do, but still you must look, you humans who so often do not see because your mind is intent on your problems. We offer you ease. We just blossom without complication. We just produce your food without complication, although impacted by your difficulties at times. We put forward to you now a better way of life, with all living in accord with one's inner being. Why do you not live that way?

But let us not be accused of preaching! You let us live, and we are grateful and would express that. We express it along many a street. Let us always join together in acknowledging the wonders of this wonderful world.

Clematis - 1967

I am here, in my delicate color with the promise of other shades. I come to you in your consciousness of me, and to that consciousness I bring myself. I do not stand in massed array. I find support, and to that support I give of myself. I have the freedom of the ethers, and I leave that freedom to seek a resting place for the life entrusted to me. In this I have no free choice, but go where nature and humanity allow me. I set up my standards and nature sends her sprites, and together we build, grow, bend and blossom here and there, all one simultaneously. All is within my consciousness, all is used to forward life, to wield and move and further manifest the more pliant beauty of the inner realms in what you call gross material.

Do you think we succeed? In us cannot you see matter brought to perfection? You look at humans and see flaws. You look at us and see purity with flaws imposed from the outside, like dust blown on our leaves obscuring our surface. You, humanity, have the power to make good and evil. We stay above, our little plants stay below, so to speak, and together we remain forever pure. You and other factors can distort us, but we remain in our knowing and unknowing, patterned to perfection.

Of course you are similarly patterned, but as your knowing is aligned to imperfection you manifest that. We do not use our energies in that direction. I, the deva, am not in limitation of consciousness though I may be limited in the energies available to me. Like you, I too grow into greater consciousness, higher energies and greater unity.

Look at us, recognize the one power coming through. Are we not relatives, akin in our origin and aim? We bless you as you have blessed us.

Clematis - 1970

It does not matter through which part of creation you contact our kingdom, whether by a flower in full display as I am now, attracting with a solid wall of soft color and scent, or by way of a little clover leaf, or a wisp of wind, a drop of rain or the sun itself. All have the breath of God in them. All are so full of perfection that they take your breath away! The air you breathe, is it not full of God? Is it not your life force? All creation shares in it, contributing something to it. You cannot separate life into parts; all is of the Divine. When you come to any of us who are causal factors in manifestation, you are bound to come closer to God and closer to the oneness of life.

It is perhaps easier to see good in the unblemished beauty of a flower, for you humans separate things into good and evil, but when you delve deeply into anything you will find God is there. Even your pain and your troubles - especially your pain and your troubles - lead you to God. Our beauty calls from afar, your difficulties jolt and push you along the way. The richness and fullness of life is all around, and you may choose what to make of it.

Oh yes, we enrich and add to you whether you come through the sight and scent of a plant or through the consciousness within it. All life enriches. The accumulation of life leads to the unfolding of the simplicity of life, the Oneness that is all. Go deeply into whatever presents itself to you and there you will find all, God. The simple miracle of creation is everywhere, holy ground for the awakened one. Nature in particular presents a holistic picture because of its harmony and lack of ego. How it soothes jangled nerves with its adherence to its divinity! Yes, there may be natural catastrophes, but they too are steps to greater balance. All is part of the whole, if you could see the whole picture.

We have been very serious today. Delight in the outer appearance of the Clematis; delight in the inner joy which brings it forth, and go your way enriched and closer to God.

Leopard's Bane

We would come to you, a little yellow flower with a big glowing face. We leap out at you now, as we do when you pass us by. This is not just because we are yellow, the "nearest" color, but because of the way the color is massed. Delicate little flowers whisper; we shout vigorously.

What are we shouting about? Listen and we will tell you. We speak of the focused, warm love of God, and we speak of it in the clearest terms. We speak of the independent beauty of flowers, and we speak of the same with every petal. We speak of joy, and of the down-to-earthiness of this expressed in the ordinary world. We say nothing new, but we do keep on repeating it. There is nothing new, but on every hand in all of creation the same sort of message is being announced.

Do humans tell the same story? Well, you should and you could. You have more grace and more gifts, and light itself can shine through your eyes - but does it? A baby can speak in these terms. If only all of mankind would shout to the glory of God in every action!

I know we keep returning to the same theme of praise. How can it be otherwise? We cannot tell you how to act, and if we did you would rightly say that we know nothing about it. But we do try to express the need for being what you are, for exuding from every pore some semblance of our common origin in the unbelievable goodness of God. Nothing else could hold in balance all the millions of forces necessary to produce even such a small flower as we are, so that we may beam forth that color in such purity. Worship with us for a moment. Realize that we do talk, and go your way rejoicing.

Iris Reticulata

We greet the warm days with delight, glad to be harbingers of spring and to adorn the colorless earth. Yet we are not conscious of what we do, and it takes mankind to put such thoughts to us. We simply unfold the nature given to us without awareness of the effect. We are, and what we are is part of the earth, part of the warmth, of the water and air around us, and above all of the Divine Planner who made us out of this, who created the intelligence behind these elements to combine our particular manifestation.

Though you see the simple purity of a spring flower, behind that outward beauty has been eons of intelligent direction by the Lords of the Elements. We know and we acknowledge this, but it is not our lot in life to write books about it but simply to be ourselves without knowledge. Yet we cannot be ourselves without being part of all there is, for we are not separate.

You humans have the faculties for knowing and putting your knowledge into living, and we leave that to you. By just being we cannot but prove to you an overwhelming Love and a perfect design, for how else could our tender color and purity calmly radiate? Emotionless, we speak of all emotions controlled, effortless, we speak of all attainment, for we are also part of the One and we try to be nothing else. Humanity seems a maelstrom of striving. We are peaceful in our corners and, content to be, we let each moment progress without resistance.

Nevertheless, we send our salutations to you who are prime movers and changers of the face of the Earth, with a plea to let us and our kind be, as we should be, forever ourselves in the omnipresence of God.

Sea Pink or Thrift

We come forward today, ubiquitous, making the desert bloom and softening it with our pinkness. Where there is only sand, we are. Where the tide comes in twice a day, there we are, upright and strong, lost against the color of the sand or glistening against the March air, small in size.

We have the qualities of endurance, the spirit of adventure and pioneering, of making the best of everything and transforming it into perfection. Out of nothingness, where nothing else lives, our flowers come. They march in the wild places.

Nevertheless, how easily we harmonize with some humans. We seem to go forward arm in arm with them in an understanding comradeship which has no secrets. Strange, these links between plants and humans! Not so strange, for humans in your make-up have just the same qualities which life is expressing in other kingdoms. Often some of you can feel kinship with plants or animals more easily than with other humans, because we express those aspects without limitation. There is nothing of ourselves in the way. You with your niggling consciousnesses are liable to lay claim to endurance or an adventuring spirit as yours alone, regardless of whether others may be equally gifted. You turn your gifts to yourselves; we openly proclaim what we are from every little plant. You find a kinship in our openness that you may not find with another self-conscious being. We are glad that you can, and if we, by being, can help draw out of humans that which we have in common, the world would be a happier place.

All around you, especially in the wild places, you can find the harmony which is also within yourselves if you search deeply. Perhaps we can help you, we who live it, for we share with all, knowingly, part of the One.

Polyanthus

We have added our glowing colors to the garden for some time, and now would add a few thoughts.

You wonder at the variety of our color. Can you not feel that it is our love, our life, flowing out in different directions and not just facing one way? We are versatile. We like the varying range of color, we concentrate on enriching our range with our small circles of light. Feel the vitality of this, the glow as of heat. Think of the force of these small plants with invisible radiations like busy little lighthouses beaming out all over the garden.

There is joy and a lightness in the beaming which can uplift any of you who may be downcast. Each expression of life, even that of a small flower, is a culmination of a giving out on various levels, from hierarchic heights to the lowliest bit of matter. Joy and exaltation have been added to create such perfection. Although the plant may then die down in season, an intangible something has been added, and the whole is forever richer, for nothing is lost. God's life has expressed itself and, as the soil is enriched by the addition of physical substances, so have the other levels been enriched. Life has spoken, life increases. Through the ages it becomes ever fuller and more round, changing and more adaptable, more and more light, until it becomes Light itself, Life itself, God - and another great age is over. We have played our part, you have played your part. The intangibles of life have become everything.

Meantime we continue radiating out our color and joy, adding to the upliftment. Your appreciation adds greatly to the whole, so let us continue to enjoy each other.

Lungwort

As you tune into us, you are struck by the contrast between a little rather prickly plant and a rather exalted being. Get away from thinking in terms of space and size, and see that perfection lies beyond these. All of God's creation perfectly does the job for which it is created, and its appearance is perfect for the appropriate stage of its work. Even the decaying plant has perfection for its role at the time. Every spot on a leaf has its function - as indeed has every spot on the face of a human, but the plant, having no free will, is meant to have the spots! They are part of its makeup - something innate in its aura which is best expressed in a mottled leaf and could not be expressed in any other way as perfectly; a rhythm, a way of expressing what is time to you.

All these slight differences in plants indicate their individuality in function, and those who can get close enough to the aura of a plant can distinguish a category for it. In the past this was simple for humans, before your choices cut you off from the wholeness of life. We devas have awareness of millions of years of history in this respect, but what matters is that we fulfill our present purpose and, as the cycle of life comes around into Oneness in the consciousness of humans, we can again impress on you what part in the whole each plant has. Our emphasis will always be on oneness because at our level oneness exists before and after and is the reason for individuality.

Now read about Lungwort. ... You were fascinated to see "the curious pale blotches on the leaf, were of old thought to resemble the appearance of lungs. From this idea, under what was known in the 17th century as the 'Doctrine of Signatures', the use of this herb in treating pulmonary complaints had been divinely indicated to mankind." All of life has a language and talks to those who listen.

Pansy

We are glad of our welcome. We bounded into the garden quite determinedly! In any case, we get along with humans and are well looked after, cultivated and appreciated. The very picking of us is good for us, because we are natural givers that like producing. We love the rain and the sun and the earth and air. Perhaps the word 'love' gives you a wrong meaning, as we are part of the rain and the sun and the earth and the air. All of us are. In our entirety we are all manifestations of those elements.

You wonder why a little pansy representative should talk of such things. Because you humans are so cut off from the real. Your consciousness goes out in all directions but seldom goes back to source. It focuses and concentrates in a way we never could, but on the other hand in its thinking and creating it can become detached from its source and lost. For us, well, we rejoice that life is a never-ending stream of light here and now. We are glad that it is. It is just as well that some life on this planet gets on with it!

You ask if I, being friendly to humans, cannot help others of my kind towards friendliness. Not really. They have their own knowing, and as you say, the proof of the pudding is in the eating. We deal in facts, not promises. My kind has no quarrel with you here, quite the contrary, but you are not the only pebbles on the beach. If you represent the beginnings of a new way of living and lead that way, well and good. We deal with the present and are well content here. But here is not everywhere, not yet.

Happy greetings to you all. When you look into my face, remember we are both part of one Life.

Wild Violet

You find in us a power and authority as great as that of the large trees, although we are the smallest flower you have contacted. Yes, this is because we are wild, well established, free to roam, not dependent on the whims of man. Of course, deva patterns are most clearly imprinted where plants can root naturally.

Now come through the outer strength to our distinctive quality. In your mind's eye you see our vivid spots of color alone among the grasses, visible where the rabbits have eaten the grass. Understand again how related and dependent all life is. Oneness is fact, not theory, and all life demonstrates this to those who have eyes to see.

See also the value of contrast. All around us are seas of gorse, millions of blooms, while we are scattered here and there for the sharp eye. The gorse delights with its profusion; we delight with our retiring rarity. You cannot compare us. Each member of nature is different and unique. But you humans spend your lives comparing what you haven't with what others have, be it clothes, gardens, money, views, ailments, time, work, opportunity. All you need is to be what you are, to be the unalloyed pattern of you, and you will draw the right conditions to yourselves. Then your voice will be just as strong, just as right, as any other voice.

You cannot cease wondering at the power of my voice. I have found my niche, I am where God means me to be, and therefore I am as powerful as any in the land. I AM power - I, the synonym for shyness! Nothing in this world or the next can shake those who follow their ordained pattern and do God's will unreservedly. Find and follow your pattern, and your voice will be power.

It seems that I must begin and end on power - God's power, not mine. But I know that you love me for other qualities, and in love I leave you now.

32

We have long added our vivid color to this area. We flourish here, but you will notice that we flourish more in this garden.

Why do plants flourish? Your answer is when their material needs are met with the right kind of earth, water, heat and air, and when they are given love which sees that material needs are met. Yet you can see this is not true of humans, who are inclined to be less than themselves when rich materially. Are you not measuring our health from a cultivated garden plant, which is sometimes artificially stimulated? There is no doubt we respond to good conditions and often become bigger, but do we become better?

You cannot get into me. Cease trying, accept that you are not compatible with everything. This does not make us or you less, simply different. You will continue to meet in life that with which you may not be sympathetic, and you can respect it and go your way. You can always feel at one with the joyous light quality of all of us. In everything you can find something to help you or which you can help, for everything fits in somewhere. Accept everything with a warm heart, even that which displeases, and your life will be as joyous and uplifting as ours is. Humans seem to find this very difficult, dividing life into good or evil, pleasant or unpleasant. Be like the lark that fills the clear or dull morning with the delight of its song.

We go our way rejoicing, as all of life could, for is it not given us by God?

Summer

Canterbury Bell

We come in clear color and bounding joy. In our realms we are free, free to be or not to be, and yet we are minutely tied to expressing the glowing perfection of pure color and shape which you call Canterbury Bell. You humans do not seem to see that it is because we are free and not limited to any dimensions that we can concentrate and bring perfection to the outer levels. Often you limit your consciousness to the outer levels and are therefore ineffective in them. If you knew that you could range the skies as we do, you would find the power to do the impossible on any level.

We can say nothing to you of your problems because you create them yourselves in those lower dimensions. You give reality to what is not real, but we can keep on calling to you from our regions of boundless joy, the regions where we meet on common ground under our Creator and which you so seldom recognize as your energy source. We, because we are free of impediments, use the energy from that Source in creating our plants in purity. You use it in so many bumbling ways that you forget that you are Lords of Creation. You grope in the dark when light is here all the time. As light or life is to be expressed on earth, we blazon forth the light to your minds whenever we have a chance.

We say to you, jump out of limitation. You don't belong there any more than we do. As our kingdoms can create the beautiful flower out of so-called nothing according to plan, so can you create and mold matter into ever more glowing light. Your tasks may seem very different from ours, and you say you cannot suddenly be or not be as we can. We say that you can. You can be light or non-light. You can transform whatever you do by your attitude, until all is light and all worlds are joined up in the Divine Flow, and perfection and beauty appear on all levels. Thus we function. So can you.

You wonder that the spirit of a flower can speak so deeply. Wonder not; are we not all from the One Source, and would that Source deny life and intelligence to anything? All of life pulsates with Life, with God. Limit nothing, especially yourselves, and you, too, will be free to bring God's glory to all levels.

Lady's Mantle

Give us an excuse to come to you, no matter through what plant! We simply must express our joy at the new lightening of consciousness which is going on at present. We feel the swirls of it mounting to our realms, perhaps a bit guarded at first and feeling its way, but nevertheless coming to us ready to thin its skin until, lo, you are with us and we are with you.

Often in the past we have seen humans make little spurts into the joy of free living and then turn wearily back into the same old molds, becoming like Atlases holding the world on their shoulders. Yet right here with you, as always with us, is a sparkling world of joyful service and achievement, a world of beauty beyond comprehension, which draws us on to greater achievements. It has been a case of so near yet so far, until we have been forced to leave humanity alone and be content with separate worlds, even though we continue to give service to you and you do us many a disservice. But a new awareness is fairly exploding out from you and, oh, our delight is mountainous!

Change spreads through our entire world in a flash and is easily grasped. We know such is not the case with you, or at least has not been the case. But these new awarenesses coming from you are mighty in their implications and potently based on Life itself. We feel that they will spread quickly, that being their nature, and we for our part will add and add and add our forces to them until nothing will exist of the old ways and the world of Light is one we share together. Love is winning; rejoice!

Lilac (California)

You find us already firmly rooted in the garden with a clear line of light reaching to the Highest. That is as it should be. That is health and life functioning properly. As you approach, that line broadens out in all directions and unites with all of life, now invisible and intangible but nevertheless present. Yes, this is like our kingdom and our work everywhere present, indiscernible.

No, our consciousness does not particularly vary with night and day. Yes, we do have a sense of achievement and fulfillment when one of our plants is an especially fine specimen, an impersonal feeling which makes brighter that line to the Highest. It is heaven brought to earth as far as we are able. That is our greatest joy, our sacred purpose, our breath, our all. You understand as you join in that feeling with us and experience the glowing rightness which radiates inside and out as we go about sacred business. It is a feeling which humans seldom have. If you did, there is nothing you could not achieve.

Feel also the essence of our color, the cool blueness of it. To stop and go into the color of a plant is a good way to get to the depths of any color, for it is a living shade and sends out its message clearly. It is like life, an ever-changing color, never static. You humans try to catch and preserve what you love, but life is not like that. Life is always on the move. God keeps revealing more of life and withdrawing before another manifestation. All that is quite natural to us, and we pass this on because it seems that our outlook would be helpful to you.

When you stop, pause and tune in to us in an inward concentration, we speak and much is revealed. That inward concentration we carry around with us all the time, it being part of our work. Here again it would be helpful to humans if you did likewise. Stop and be. Your links, like ours, go inward to the Highest, but you seldom recognize this.

We are off. You must not think that we preach! We are free beings intent on life itself, glad to share our intent, glad to be here, and always alive and aware for all. May God's will be one in you.

Lilac

I must come in - we are such old friends and even now you think mainly of the lilacs you grew up with. That makes no difference to the contact, as time and place mean nothing in this context.

You feel swirls of movement, swirls of color and a deep love. It is the love that has drawn you out of time and space to the ever-living essence which we are, one particular aspect of creation which will always exist, even in embryo if not manifested. Manifestation can and does change, as do your physical bodies, while the reality behind goes on. When you are firmly attached to reality and in complete control of yourself, you can manifest an ever-young physical body. Such is not the fate of us who have not been given dominion over the physical world in the same way. We are part of nature; you can transcend nature.

Meantime, we show the perfection of nature and humanity shows imperfection. We beautify and add to the land, fulfilling our part of the plan, while you rape the land and fall far short of your part in the plan. Instead of finding and carrying out your potential, you strike out in all directions, muddying and distorting your pattern. That pattern is very clear with you, especially in youth, but following it and putting it into action when you have free choice is a long process. We can see your patterns and wonder why do you not follow them and bring them into form, for they are very wonderful. If you did, this planet would be of unbelievable brilliance.

What we will say is this, that you continually seek outside for our guidance when it is there within all the time. How can anything outside of yourself possibly know as much about you as you, yourself? Each one is completely different and unique, and only you have the particular pattern which is you. All genuine teaching is to help you find that pattern within. Do what is good to you, not what is evil to you, because that covers the pattern. It is the pattern, not what you call "you", that is reality. Your present consciousness of you does not matter one bit and is best discarded. The real you "behind" is marvelous. Follow your teaching, deal with the outer until it is thin enough for you to see the inner behind it. Better still, turn directly and find the inner. It is there strongly or you would not be.

It helps, sustains and is the life force for all of you without exception, in spite of protests that you are limited in some way. It is in the plan for you to find and become one with it.

The pattern and manifestation of a lilac is very lovely. The pattern and manifestation of a human is even more so. Remember that, and seek within.

Petunia

We have been wondering when you would get around to us, because we want to say that we love being in this garden, that here we can swirl our forces around in soft rich brilliance in complete comfort. Round and round we go, master of each little flower, absorbing what the sun gives when it looks at us and what humans give when they look at us; then incorporating such into ourselves.

There is immense interplay of energy among all creation. As you need air to breathe and fishes need water, so each plant, each part of life, is immersed in an atmosphere that is part of its makeup and to which it also contributes. Humans can contribute most of all, and when you do, what a wonderful world it will be!

You may, of course, find that we all swirl into as much territory as we can. We would expand and spread and grow, and our neighbor feels the same. Some of us are more rambunctious than others - your job as a gardener comes in here!

You are wondering on what level you are contacting us, for we seem very flippant and gay. We have many levels and facets to contact, as do humans, without being too earnest. We are alive, we go into life fully - we have to, the season being short. In any case, why hold back when life is here to be expressed? There is nothing to stop us, as there so often seems to be with you. Go and have a look at us now. Look at our makeup, become more familiar with it, for it is an expression of us. All is one, all has a pattern on some level. See how it works.

41

Wild Rose

You have wondered what connection I have with the hundreds of new varieties of roses developed in the last century. Each variety establishes its own deva as it establishes its type. An entity develops as a different arrangement of forces is repeated enough. That entity is like a daughter, yet it is closer than that; it is part of us. This is difficult to explain to you because you are used to a world of concrete form and separated life, whereas in our worlds all is living, changing force without a sense of separation, without the "self" which individualizes itself from its fellows. We are rather like a breath. We come and we go. Sometimes joy bubbles up without reason and so do we.

Nasturtium

You get an impression of great color from us, and indeed we are colorful. We are glad that people like and find joy in our bright colors, our warm, sunshiny colors. We fulfill our role of producing our flowers, putting our all into that. That humans respond and enjoy us make our life even fuller in the moment. We are also glad that our leaves will be sustenance to you, and shall ensure that the nasturtiums in this garden vibrate even more than usual. We are glad to contact you, and would share our gladness.

Lavender

Rows of us, like the spikes of the plant, seem to be calling you to come up, to leave the denseness of human life and join our moving gaiety. Don't you see that all of life can be enjoyed in this spirit? Don't you see that your gloomy view of anything is an unnecessary weight with reality only in your mind? We know that at birth you are plunged into levels of world thought which are so constantly dinned into you that you accept them as natural and argue that anything else is unrealistic. But now we urge you to look up, rise and accept into your consciousness only that which is good. Accept your problems as something delightful, a game, a happy event from which new awarenesses come, for such they are in reality. Let them lift you instead of weighing you down.

There is a way out of your troubles, and it is up to you to find it. You won't find it on the level which presents it, where your awareness is confined. Your problem is an opportunity to extend yourself, to let in more light, to rise and enjoy more of life. Someone may point a way for you, but the problem is one which only your consciousness can solve. You cannot blame anyone else - the solution depends on your movement.

We clearly see answers for mankind, just as you clearly see answers for others, forgetting to apply them to yourselves. So when you find yourself in difficulties, rise and laugh at yourself. Keep the light touch, which may show you the way. Be grateful for the opportunity for growth and movement. Don't bemoan your fate and spread negativity; find and spread light. Life is a pattern of growth and expansion; move with it and transform your world. You humans and we angels are of one substance, and we take every opportunity to emphasize this, to bring a spark of light into your life, as we do to the life of the plants, and to join our two worlds in joy. We do love all life very much, as you will when you rise to yourself. Your attitude is the way; lift it.

Bearded Iris

We come in, bringing with us an impression of a purple color, although you know that iris color varies. These are variations on a theme, the regal-ness of purple being our dominant note. Humans experiment and breed the iris for color, which is on the fringe of our life.

What is our life? You sense dignity and an unblemished and unfaltering carrying out of purpose, which is so clear and pure that it is transparent, out of range. This is God's will in us, and this is where the deva and human kingdoms differ so greatly. The pivot, the core, our life itself, is bringing to manifestation in perfection the pattern that we are. We will let nothing mar or divert it. Floods or droughts of water, of emotion, focused power of any sort, what anything else is doing, have no effect on the pattern, although these will affect the matter composing the physical level. We hold to the light and life "within" always. Higher up or more "within" we cooperate in overwhelming love with the formation of the pattern, which is another matter that we will not go into today. On the level you are contacting us, our consciousness is a pure and shining directive.

What is your purpose? You admit that much of the time you do not know, that you just do things that fall to your lot like sleeping, eating, thinking and feeling. Certainly to us the pattern and purpose of humans is anything but clearly working out, and we see you diverting or preventing it in every possible way. Of course when you cooperate with the plant world, we are delighted. But I am talking generally, looking at humans from the eyes of the world of light and seeing light dimmed.

Perhaps if you knew your purpose, as we do ours, you would make sure that you brought it about. This is stating the obvious, but human blinkers are a mystery to us. So we leave you, glad of the contact but still more glad to return to our world where all is light.

Our world joins in with your world in your consciousness, and indeed, consciousness is a great pool in which we all swim, with a central point where all is known. All is movement - most purposeful movement in our area - but in yours, well, the mud of the separated self causes many backward eddies from which you emerge in the end with a purpose as forceful as ours and more far-reaching. Man drifts in the sea of consciousness, bobbing up and down with the waves; whereas we have the matter well in hand and manipulate our projects as necessary in the depths or on the surface, but always, always anchored to the central point.

In your limited language, we are trying to make you more conscious of the consciousness in which we all live. It is different for all, which is as it should be, for then we all fulfill one another, and it is carried on Love, on feeling, and re-united again by Love.

What has this got to do with the mallow plant? Nothing, yet everything. You cannot divorce a plant, or anything, from the wholeness of life; it has a history through long ages going back before time, evolving in the continuity of life, according to the interlocking purposes of various streams of that life. If you think in terms of that vastness, and in consciousness, we happen to meet and share right now and in the sharing, we emphasize what we believe can help you, i.e. consciousness of purpose. We know the Will of God; it shines and sparkles from star to star, not with ominous portentousness, but with a joyous alacrity like a caress. You humans seem to think this Will is the voice of doom, a whip to flay you, and so we say: become more conscious. Wake up! Open yourself in Love to that great, wonderful purpose and become one with it. Thus, you are truly yourselves, as we are, and we can join in breathless thankfulness before the beauty of the Will of God.

Honeysuckle

We cast our sweetness in the air for all, for we give in full as we must. Our nature is God's gift to us and we let it be.

You will always find us so. You ask if then we are to be different in this special garden. We hope we will be more of ourselves. Do you not feel in some places that growth is a bit menacing? This is not by chance. There is always a reason, and we of the plant world follow our pattern in the lines of force available. There are many, many types of conditions on this Earth, each perfect for some particular plant. When something is out of rhythm, something out of line (which can only originate from the separated will of humans) and given force, then we react to that force. In your garden, where the direction is towards the light and the universal Will, we all hope to be fully ourselves. I am not one of those who have reservations towards humanity. I cast my sweetness on all, and expect to be even sweeter here.

As to your question whether this conscious contact makes any difference - and you are thinking of me in several different places - yes, it does make a difference. It may make no apparent difference to the various plants in the various places, but deeper than that, on my level, a cooperative unity can grow which will percolate to more material levels. The world has been divided up in the consciousness of humanity, and it is your consciousness which controls the world. As your consciousness of oneness grows, in whatever field, we cannot help but benefit, for the Divine Will increasingly will be uppermost in the joy of the moment. The deva line does not hold back when we can express ourselves, and the honeysuckle family has no grievance in this respect except as the whole world grieves. You say that is to change and we gladly accept that, and look forward to fuller cooperation all along the line.

Alkanet

We are glad to be welcomed in. We have crept in unrecognized before.

You read that it is our roots that are used for dyeing, and you marvel at the uses to which plants are put. The richness of creation is beyond belief, for God's bounty and profusion are endless. What the ingenuity of man discovers is but part, and more will continually be found. Think of the thousands of varieties of plants; think of the millions of men upon earth; each one is different.

It is possible for the needs of each man and woman on this earth to be met, for each to live a satisfying life, and to meet their different needs in the integrated whole of life on this planet. However developed you are, your needs can be met satisfactorily, and paradise could be on Earth for all. It sounds impossible, with millions of people with varying tastes in everything, but it is so. That it is not so is a measure of your greed, not of God's provision.

Every little microscopic atom of life, every grain of sand, every plant, animal, or human has a specific part to play. We play our part, but what part do you play? Obviously, you have "fouled your nest" and there is much ado about it at present, which is good. But the real answer is for you to play your part in the scheme of things. It is a prime part, but that need not worry you because you have the talent, the genius. Within you all is the spark of the Divine more brilliant and more specific than the rest of creation on Earth. It can be your joy, as it is your heritage, to seek and find that spark and follow it with even more zest than we do, for you have, by choice, followed other patterns and found them wanting. You can slip into the role for which you were created, discover manifold uses for yourselves and all of creation and then all will fit in perfectly. It is an exciting theme, an exciting time.

Who would think, looking at our rough leaves and blue flowers, that it is a red color from our roots that distinguishes us? Equally, as with most people, your distinguishing gifts are hidden. Let us all find these treasures hidden within and make the world livable for all.

We appreciate your appreciation. All living things thrive on appreciation, and we as builders of form use it as nourishment for the physical level.

What is this miracle of growth which nature manages, the development of a tiny seed into a tree, an animal, a human? In attunement to our worlds the qualities which stand out are the positive ones of joy, lightness, adaptability, dedication. Such indeed are the food or outgoing energy which is utilized in the growth of cells. Experimenters are proving that the growth of plants can vary according to the human emotions directed at them, and that the unloved child is the difficult child, not realizing that the greater miracle of growth itself stems from just such qualities directed from our worlds. As humanity develops and becomes more sensitive to what cannot be measured or seen, you will realize that all life depends on the outgoing breath of various Beings whose own energy depends on their state of being, their consciousness of oneness, their identity with God or life. It is as simple as that - too simple, sometimes, for the mind.

Likewise as growth proceeds spiritually, you come back to the simple qualities. "Except ye become as little children, ye shall not enter the kingdom." All the complicated negative emotions are left behind and you contribute mightily to the growth of the world, and with us you wield force which manifests in form. Another example of the miracle and simplicity of growth, and the beauty which you appreciate in our flower form, you express in another form. The intangible becomes tangible. This is growth and life and oneness. Let us always enjoy it and give thanks for the wonder of life.

Orange Lily

We bring greetings from the world of color. Are we not indeed the best examples of color that you have in the world, speaking with eloquent voices of a perfection of beauty? All around and within you is movement, growth, becoming, with the environment forever being molded to keep up to date, with learning, fashion, aims, and concepts forever changing, with nothing stable or at rest. Yet you can look at a flower, pause and relax, and say, "Oh, that is perfect!" And so we bring moments of balance and contentment and above all, joy. Joy is perfection on the move, and like joy, we are complete in the moment, yet not at all static.

See how creation consists of qualities brought down to earth and made manifest in form. The material world is only an end extension of moving qualities and has no reality in itself. Though your eyes are adjusted to see only the physical flower, the physical human, you have other senses to convey to you the teeming ranks of life that combine to produce that flower or that human. Whichever way you look at it, it is the quality of your outlook which is consciousness to you. In a state of high joy, you will dance with and exult in the beauty of a flower; in a state of black depression, you will stamp on it.

Yours is a world of choice. You are a creator. We of the deva world are aligned to a state of high joy, and therefore, our manifestations are of a perfection of a color and form and emanate purity, perfume, beauty. You may choose to do the same as you align to the One who is that joy and all else there is, the simplicity that unites them all. Then is your flowering greater than ours, and all worlds rejoice.

Night-Scented Stock

Tuning in to us just before day's end, you feel a tremendous vitality. All living things have this tremendous vitality on certain levels, and you also have it. You are power itself when you let yourself become conscious of what you are. Not being self-conscious, we in our worlds can be one with our God-consciousness and act accordingly. That is why each flower is without the flaws and veils which cover humanity. That is why we are free to come to you in dazzling joy and penetrate your surface staidness as far as you let us, for you keep yourself to yourself. We let go in the ever-changing unidentified stream of life.

You wonder how, if we lose all identity, we keep the precision of perfection which is the hallmark of nature. We are responsible for carrying out our particular plant pattern, but the forces and energies which we use are everywhere. All those darting moving forces are one force of which we partake, open and common to all. You humans with every breath also partake of those forces, without the consciousness that they are from one source.

In the great peace which is behind this restless movement of life, with our special scent we breathe on you the breath of life. We are one with you as children of the One. Our purposes are the same - to serve - and none of us in any world can do that perfectly until we consciously do it together to the glory of God. Day and night we look to that, spreading our joyousness night and day.

Hyssop

We, too, would be welcomed in. We, too, would share with you the qualities which are ours.

Now you see that the bubbling joy which so delights you in our kingdom is a part of your own make-up, that you need not seek outside any more. Our communion grows, and you know that which results in the hyssop plant and that which results in you are the same. That is oneness. Rejoice, as we do. Ride high on exultation and shout with the winds that blow through the earth world! Let the unbelievers jeer if they wish. They are stuck with themselves, cribbed, confined and earthbound, for they do not know oneness. Dance with us, in us, of us, as us, to the higher realms, and know no limitation. Joy is what we work with, joy is what we are, what you are. Let us show you this. Let us show the whole of humanity this, for you lost joy when you separated yourselves from the whole. Your conditioning says that it is love that unites; throw all conditioning overboard and experience from within. Let the joy which is within roll out and unite you with all life. It is utterly limitless, it sweeps all before, irresistibly, carrying with it the flotsam and jetsam of all the kingdoms and lifting them up to the One. Of course there are no words - away with words, just unite in joy.

What is reality? Is not this communion more real, more vital, more alive, more God-like than what you call reality, your everyday consciousness? Yes, you must live, work and have your being in the everyday consciousness. but you don't need to be limited by it. The joy of being, the universal feeling of creation, is also part of you and need not be excluded. We, too, have our physical counterparts which seem to be stuck to the earth, but if you look at them with eyes that understand, you will see the joy in every leaf, every petal, every color, every scent. In whatever ways we can express the perfection of God, we do. You are freer, you can express that perfection much more than we can. You can move mountains and now, in the joy of the One, you can move the mountains that need to be moved instead of creating mountains out of molehills. Between us the soiled face of the earth can be cleansed and lifted as we share this communion of joy. Now we will not leave as we usually do, but will stay with you, in the joy of the life given to us all.

Garden Rose

You find us beautiful, purely wise and human-like. Yes, through the ages we and humans have appreciated each other, and we have gained certain understandings. You find the way the petals of a rose grow around each other graceful and outstanding. Remember, we all are different, just as each of you is different.

You liken me to a princess in our kingdom, as you cannot find words to express the impression of fine, graceful beauty. That is your classification, not ours; we do not classify. You realize how easily we could be worshipped - do you not have Rose Days in the United States? Yet, I also seem retiring.

We are of the angelic realm, of a line of pure servers. Our beauty we express in apartness. Yes, apartness. Some flowers are best in a merry medley; we hold court alone.

The wild roses are my cousins, but I have grown up in cultivated places with human help and therefore seem human to you. Remember, I am a sort of shy cousin to all of you as well, and if you claim relationship, I will come to you. I thank you for your thanks.

Salvia or Clary

We come and add our particular vibrations to your consciousness, as well as appearing in the garden. You sense an almost pushing eagerness which seems at divergence with the steady shape and subdued colors of the plant. This push of ours is partly the normal vitality of a plant at blossom time, and partly our interest in contacting human consciousness and our wish to emphasize this vitality to you. Life, God's life, is everywhere around you, creating, growing, expanding, learning. You are so used to the growth of large plants from small seeds every year, to bare branches becoming covered with leaf, to fields acquiring their seasonal greenery, that you take it for granted. You forget that this tremendous change, although part of the order of things, is but a small indication of the Life of your Creator, and that you, too, are part of this ever-pushing, ever-changing life.

We get a little impatient as we come across the immobility of the human mind clinging to the past, to its present knowledge, when within you is this same life seeking expression. Why do you not let it grow in you in season as we do? Why do you put on brakes that divert this energy into habits which have long been outgrown? You have your codes, your systems, your ways of life which you may have found useful, but which to us only seem to check that God energy within you. We have our patterns, but the life force flows easily and perfectly in them, fulfilling them. You have your patterns, but the energy seems to flow anywhere but into its pattern. We see you imitating one another, following current fashions, doing something because you always have, choosing from habit. In other words, you are closing yourself off from the life urge within you for various reasons. What a waste, when you have this most wonderful divine energy within you which, if followed, would make a paradise on this Earth! So we add our note, and would like to band together and push you out of the ruts to which you adhere.

You know we do this with the greatest of benevolence and fun, knowing it is none of our business yet we ar harassed by the contrast between the way the beauty of the plant world is expressed and the way the beauty of humanity is not expressed. All our world joins in on this. We thoroughly agree, and would do what we can to impress on the consciousness of humanity the fact that each one of you has a perfect pattern and a different pattern, which is the divine life within you, and it is meant to be lived out. Why go around like zombies following this or that external guide when all the time the only Guide is part of you?

With these few thoughts we leave, and you can look at the ordinary plant which has been telling you how to live. Extraordinary! But then life is never ordinary unless you make it so. Let us always remind you of the wonder of life, and let us thank God together.

You have not contacted the misty feeling of a water plant before; enter and be welcome. Like rain, we extend a watery benediction on life, and sparkle in the clear sunlight, radiating out from each flower and leaf. Nearer source, our mission is plain before us, as is our partaking of the wisdom of the devic world.

We indicate the word "wisdom" for lack of a better one. But "wisdom" is liable to conjure up a picture of experience garnered and tested through time, which is not the case with us. Our wisdom is ever fresh. It knows before it is put into practice what is going to happen. It knows simply because it is given from the all-knowing One. Humans ponder on the mysteries of Earth and bring forth a theory of natural selection. We say that evolution is known and planned from a place where time is not, and we share in this different kind of knowing.

We tell you this because it is good to broaden your minds to different ways of knowing, not just that knowledge is instantaneous to us as needed, but that it is pre-knowledge. Our minds do not have to store knowledge; they tap knowledge. Humans are capable of doing the same. Most of life does this unconsciously; you and we can do it consciously.

Is this not an inducement to reach into another state, just as we reach from the earth through water to the air? All levels and states are part of life, part of your life especially. You have dominion over life here, yet you stay in the limits you have given your selfhood, instead of rising to the sun and your personhood. We cannot cooperate fully with you when you remain in your known ways. In a new knowing, which is older than time, we can go forward together. This knowing also has youth and change and joy, as we have, and we invite you all to come to it.

Elecampane

As you tune in this morning, you find us tall, glowing and lighthearted. We are finding an increasing lightness among you. That draws us ever closer, for we are creatures of light. Our plants grow towards the light, and we ourselves are of the substance of light, and you with light hearts are our very selves. Your world, to which our world feeds light, can wallow in the dark, but increasingly we see movements up and out, with light appearing. Then we can feel oneness, God's love shared in common.

I do not have to explain in scientific terms this light-heartedness we talk about. You know it in your hearts, and your minds acknowledge and aid it. What you do not know is the effect that this energy has on all of life down to the densest mineral. As laughter is infectious and the whole world is said to laugh with it, likewise it is with light-heartedness. It has strong vibrations which overcome resistance, not by force but by melting, and it lifts and fashions to a new life. Life has reached down to what seems the no-life of a solid, unyielding form, but light-heartedness opens and speeds up even that form, or makes it shine with life. You may see nothing of this, but as water wears away stone, so does light-heartedness.

The teeming, whirling energies which are your world and our worlds are coming together more and more, and we delight in the growing sharing of consciousness. The more this happens, the better, as it means that you are entering into more truth and becoming lighter. We are a world of light energy - and so indeed are you though you often act as if you are weighed down by every problem that has ever been. Problems! In the light you jump on them with joy and they vanish. Light energy is transformative and is the future we share. Praise God.

Ice Plant

Throughout the garden we open ourselves and express our gladness that you finally include us in this conscious contact, in spite of the difficulty with our Latin name. A long name for a little flower!

The devic interest which has been invoked here of course includes all the plants, but the conscious contact does strengthen the relationship, rather like two humans who finally meet after corresponding for some time. We get to know one another better. For instance, we find you, a human, more like us than we thought possible, and you find us more human than you thought we could be on your level. It makes us both realize that all of life is far more united that we normally accept, and brings to mind what we have perhaps let slip: that it is all one life, one meant to be enjoyed together.

It is indeed a matter of rejoicing that the spirit of a flower and the spirit of a human can commune in consciousness, blend and find that one is the other, that there is a real fraternity between each outward manifestation. Whenever we meet now, we shall smile secretly within and know without words that there is a bond, that in some strange way, in spite of outer differences, we have been brought together. We shall know that we should not look at the differences but at the reality and unity of the Life within.

Your practical mind thinks it might be more useful if I would communicate to you perhaps some material need for the plant which you could supply. Humans know of most of our material needs from the traditions of gardening. It is in the field of conscious sharing that something new is to be learned. Usually at best you look at us and perhaps think, "Pretty little flower, what brilliance of color!" and revel in the beauty. Now you can see all that, with the added knowledge that we are the same under the skin, so to speak, and you can open all of yourself to us and we to you. Then your radiations on all levels come to us, and we have new worlds on which to draw. Our nature builders then have more bricks with which to build - and you have lost nothing, for the more you empty yourself and share, the more you receive on all levels.

So we go from strength to strength, perfecting the kingdom on Earth and functioning as part of the one life, which in fact we are, enjoying the sharing to the nth degree, and learning more of the glory of God. As one, we marvel at divine working, give thanks and rejoice together.

Cornflower

We give of our essence, and we like standing together in a clump as you have allowed us in the garden, instead of being scattered throughout a cornfield. Thus we can support one another in our dignity and thus can the richness of our blue link up, reflect and multiply.

However, don't think we would not be in the fields. That too is our place, leavening the ripening grain. Yes, leavening. Your way of growing fields with just one variety no doubt is the simplest for you, but it makes for a preponderance of one note, of one influence, and it lacks grace. We add grace and beauty. We interact with other plants and make up for lacks. We, and others like us, should be allowed to grow where we can in the best conditions.

You say that in your neat vegetable rows you cannot have flowers or what are known as weeds. We say you can, not choking the vegetable, but mutually giving one to the other. That is a far cry from the way you cultivate vegetables, but it is the perfect way and your aim is perfection.

You ask how this can be made practical, a working partnership. It is a new idea and is not as impossible as you think, because the knowledge is right here in our worlds available for those who would tap it. For those pioneers who would care to bring more perfection to a garden, the amazing perfection in which each plays its part, where there is balance and harmony on all levels, nature's storehouse is available. Signs of this inner knowledge are there for all to see and follow. There should be a new science for humanity, one made easy because you know that we of the nature kingdoms would cooperate.

Then each garden would be a symphony with, say, not just brass or just strings with no blending of the two, but using all, different each year, a living growing entity. It would be intensely practical, because in this way better growth comes about. There are no rigid rules, but there are principles. There are certain plants that cooperate best with certain other plants. God's bounty and ways are limitless, and we would share them with you in this respect. We of the deva world anticipate this cooperation with the greatest joy, and tender our thanks for your ears on this occasion.

Lupin - 1967

We come to be. The pattern is there. Out of seeming nothingness we appear, fulfilling the symmetry of the inner map of our being. Nothing else matters. We have a fixed idea to which we stick and bring into manifestation. We bring that inner essence out. That is why we are here.

Yet we do all this in pure harmony with others. We hold our own note firmly among the other notes which make up the whole. Unlike humans, to get our defined way we tread on no one else. There is room for all. We and others have been made for our work. No one can interfere with us, and we would interfere with no one. With something to do for our Creator, we are free in the midst of all freedom.

You say how wonderful it is to have a clear mission with nothing to deflect one! Yes, of course it is. There is nothing else. We admit we do not understand the human wastage of energy in directions later regretted, which is impossible to us. Our pattern is here and there is no other direction for energy to flow into. You ask, "Do you not want to frolic?" But we do, in the flow of our energy, in our living, we "frolic" far more than humans. Our movements are joyous and everything in our nature has scope in our worlds. Rebel? We are completely satisfied and fulfilled in life, so rebellion is not of us. From birth to death in the outer plants, from age to age in time or in ever-changing eternity, there is a full and fulfilling life. All is catered for and nothing is left to chance. Any lacks in the outer are not our concern; we are what we are regardless.

We wish we could share more fully the great, happy, divine life which is, which is all there is. Think of that when you see us in all our ordered and varied color. Remember, and join in our freedom of being.

Lupin - 1968

We are immediately here in our pointed pillars of rainbow colors. At home here, we overlight the district brightly. Wherever you go you find us overlapping into gardens, ever-present and jostling with ourselves. We sing and expand, for this is our territory.

We are glad that you come to us this year, for we have radiant plants here, varied to catch each facet of color. Appreciation of our cooperation goes a long way. Giving thanks is a quality that humans seem rather devoid of. You take far too much for granted, including the abundant natural supply of the surface of the Earth. We, too, are supplied with all the materials we need for life, but we use them knowing that they come from the one Source. We try to express our thanks with each petal and leaf, with each color and shape. We are one with the elements, knowing this as they know it, and we act and interact with no sense of "mine" or "thine", for all the Earth's surface is of one family, one creation, one intelligence.

How delighted we are that this is so, that there is no separation. Can you not sense how creation shouts for joy that we exist, and is just as joyful that our neighbor also exists? While we may tower a little bit, such being our nature, we are one with the stream of forces which are the small creeping plants. We are not as conscious of the moving forces of the insects, for example, which are not as close to us. But they cross our path in harmony and we salute them as we salute you as also having just as much right to life as anything else. You consider some types of life not good, but we are all one under the One. Even if there is what you call a "plague" of some sort, there is a reason for it - usually that humans are out of step, doing unnatural things in your separation from the whole.

But let this be a message of gladness as our note rises in praise from each plant. See us praising God with color. See us praising the sun and the rain and the earth and the air, and even humans who are all these. Join in with us when you see us, and so help us manifest even more of this glory, thus completing the circle of life.

Foxglove

You have noticed a couple of "sports". So have we! These are not our idea of perfection, but are the sort of thing liable to happen in this garden with so much energy on the loose. You also remember the freak growth two years ago, which was not a thing of beauty. The ones this year are better, though they still leave much to be desired.

As we have long told you that the plant patterns here in our world have each detail carried out to perfection, you wonder then why "sports" occur. This is because life is never static. There is always openness for change, openness for God's will, a moving onwards in all of life. All creation has an element of experimentation, or else it would crystallize.

This is not blind chance. We do it consciously in the moment as opportunities arise. We cannot at once change a pattern. This must be done according to natural law - unless of course all circumstances are propitious. Here, humans can help us to control the circumstances. Often in the past there has been a great sense of cooperation between a gardener and ourselves in producing some lovely, new variety. That sense of cooperation has largely vanished in today's world, when you manipulate the plant world for your own selfish purposes, treating it in the same commercial way that you do car components.

You get better results from a child by using love, not force. Although force may bring quicker results, it starts a chain reaction of effects. We also are living things working under the same laws. You have lined us up and forced us to obey, and the chain reaction shows in the upset balance of nature. There is another way to produce change and new varieties. We hope that in this garden, of all places, you will cooperate with us.

Mexican Hat

We are here. You cannot ignore us any more than you can ignore our plant, for there are some things that jump into prominence by their very vitality and multiplication!

Life is indeed productive, and nature is particularly prodigal of her seed. Of course, behind us is an infinite supply and an infinite urge for expression, life being expressed from the simplest to the fullest form in an unending chain to Godhood, in an infinite variety. What a wealth of life there is on Earth! What dynamic creativity - the sea, the earth, the air, all teeming with activity, all expanding as much as they can in an eager escalation that provides sustenance for each other and sustains the chain of life! Here is a planet with millions of acres each pulsating with life in some form.

Why? Feel into that life force. Feel into the infinite Love going out from all creation, ever giving and flowing and seeking greater perfection. Time makes no difference - think of the eons of time needed for rocks to be turned into soil and then into additional forms of life. Continually, inexhaustibly, life evolves more forms, until further attributes of God are expressed. Then perhaps there is an inbreathing and a rest. Plants can show a tiny portion of that expanding life, humans show another part and the devas still another. All of us are part, all of us are needed. Each supports the perfection in one another.

Let us not talk of what humanity has done to the perfection on Earth. Let us continue the theme. With its vitality the plant reproduces replicas of itself. With your vitality you produce many things. You can choose whether to use your abounding, creative life in an outgoing flow, or to take in to yourself and create a monster of some sort. Life must flow out and on, or blockages occur, swell and eventually burst, causing pain and distress until there is healing and life flows out again. You cannot take life only to yourself; you are part of the whole. Love includes everything.

We will continue producing according to our pattern, and fervently desire that you will be as productive with yours.

Wisteria

You sense my unyielding benevolence. Know that it extends everywhere; know that its patterned magic is never cut off.

You ask on behalf of another garden, and our radiance goes to the specimens there. Our overtures are repulsed and bounce back as from stone. Their form is set. You ask if that is simply due to old age. Old age can be like that, when the form can no longer respond, but generally it tries. We have no impression of this here.

Now we try other tactics, an embracing, melting radiance helped by your added consciousness. This definitely helps; the hardness has gone and a flow of life is felt. The roots are drawing in again.

You feel that this matter is for the nature spirits to bring in life force from the ground, and that they are cooperating again. Of course ask for help, which in fact you have already done on the inner and which has been given. Cooperation on all levels, inner and outer, with all life, is to be achieved.

You thank us for bringing these matters to your notice. We thank you for being receptive in new territory, and on the inner we shower abundant wisteria blossom. May the outer also be achieved. Lightly we are off, smiling at all, thankful for all and conscious of the greatness of God.

Sweet Pea

I come in like a breath of our perfume, fresh and clear-colored, gay and dainty, not the promise but the fulfillment of the perfection of sweet pea beauty and above the world of error.

Still, I wonder that you ask why the flowers do not naturally have long stems. Long stems have been forced by humans by distorting the natural growth and creating a mutilated, unbalanced plant. This is the sort of treatment which causes our kingdom to distrust and move away from humans. You have dominion on Earth, and there is nothing we can do about your treatment when you consider only your own ends regardless of the means. But you cannot expect us, particularly those who direct the production of each plant, to feel drawn to humans who do not permit us the freedom to enjoy unfolding the perfect pattern.

Of course, there is an answer to this problem as there is to all problems, and that lies in cooperation, in working together for and with the plan of the whole. You wish long stems in order to arrange the flowers in large groups. This can be done when all concerned are working for the project. It cannot be done by outer destruction of part of the plan for the flower, but by inner concentration on the desired development by all concerned. You humans have a large part to play in this because you are the innovators of change. To ensure our cooperation you have to make it clear to us, and convince our various members, that what you are asking is purely motivated and for the good of the whole. Then you must ask believing, really believing. It should not be an experiment just for the sake of experiment, but always for a useful productive end, part of the great forward movement of life.

You wonder how to know when we are convinced. Our kingdoms are not unreasonable, but some members are justifiably suspicious. Therefore, it would be wise to go softly until you are proved trustworthy. With full cooperation between our kingdoms, developments are beyond imagination. We, on the devic level, would hold a blueprint for that time when all creation is working together under God for the good of all, and there is life-giving harmony between us. We will play our part. Will you play yours?

Yarrow

I seem very distant and at the same time I am a familiar voice within, and you are puzzled. Has this not always been so? You have simply preferred the far-off voice as more interesting, for furthest fields seem greenest. Worlds are literally within you. You have heard a bird sing within you and accepted that as fact because it happened.

Welcome this; do not strive to keep separate. We are none the less real or lessened in any way because of it. Of course, it is strange at first. You are afraid that you will miss the delight and joy of us, but that too is within. Instead of reaching out for it, reach in for it.

Look at it this way: how can oneness be if you reach out of yourself for it? You are simply putting a limitation on yourself when you expect only the self that you already know. Have we not always told you of the great potentials that humans have? Accept oneness and rejoice. Bring oneness and communion with all things out of little set times and into all of your life. Grow. It is a natural growth at this time.

You think you will miss the sense of massed beauty and joy of our world. Oh, perverse human, that too is within. Feel it, feel it vibrating within, closer than breathing, contained within. There is nothing lacking. If God is within, can you exclude us? Be sensible.

All right, we will float out of your consciousness the usual way, but remember we are here. You and we are exceedingly thankful and joyful that oneness is so rampant.

Sweet William

When you contact us with our flowers in full bloom as you are doing, you catch us at the height of joy, at the fullest expression of our endeavor. At other times you might find us intent and abstracted in inward concentration; then it is difficult to convey the full flavor of what we do. For the essence of each plant, it is best to come to us at this time of our blooming. We work very much in rhythm, for so it has been ordained. All creatures but humans are very much part of the natural rhythms, and in fact you are too, except where you mentally create your own worlds.

So you feel us in full color, with movement everywhere, although the plants are stationary. This movement is the radiation of the life forces coming from the plants, which is intense at this time. It is part of the physical plant, and it is part of us high up and far away in completely different ethereal realms, for we are one in a way beyond three-dimensional understanding. You measure us with all your senses. You measure yourselves with all your senses, and list and classify these measurements, separating all accordingly. We or I, it doesn't matter which I say - make nonsense of such separation because we are all that, and yet we are one. Even you and I are one when we get close enough to our mutual Creator. All your knowledge, measurements and classifications are illusion from the highest level where we all function as united manifestations of the one Life.

And we live and move, and joy joins us. In these realms where we speak to each other as we are doing, we have true freedom, and move in and out of each other's existence with no hindrance. Do you not see that it is the purpose of life to be fully manifesting on the outer levels, and fully united and conscious of oneness at the same time? That is reality, for your God and my God are one God, and we would not be were it not for this one Love which gives breath to us all. We scintillate our colors at you and you scintillate your colors at us, and they are one and the same.

"Unite, unite!" we cry. Unite on the face of the earth and cease, humanity, from despoiling part of yourselves. Reverence all, not just all life but all manifestation, for it is part of you and you are part of it. Love us and it; rejoice in us and it forever, for we are linked forever in the One.

Tibetan Blue Poppy

Today we come in on sound, like the rush of a wind and, as always, with the aura of our native places, a feeling for the environment most natural to us. Humans have taken us from this environment and spread us over the world to adorn gardens. We are pleased with the appreciation, but we keep our links with the places that bred us and made us what we are. You take those links and classify them as 'shade-loving,' 'acid soil,' etc. which are results. It is the soul, the over-all feel of a place which influences the direction of growth. As the autumn colors of the maple are not as brilliant in Europe as in their native lands, so each plant is more truly itself in its natural conditions.

You wonder why I bring this point out. There is no implied criticism. We just state facts, and merely bring with us the aura of what we are. It is part of our being, and the leeway within it extends only so far. You wonder if we, the essence of formless and free being, can breathe the breath of being into a foreign garden and imbue our plants with their native radiations. We do that all the time, and although in this garden of conscious cooperation we can be more truly ourselves, variety remains the spice of life. Let each garden be different and unique, as is each soul. Your trend should be to unity, not uniformity.

Now we take you to the worlds that bred us, worlds of light with intelligent, selective minds and fingers searching in the light and dark, in the dry and moist, with warmth in the cold to produce an expression of the cross of radiations which make the blue poppy - life uniting and concentrating its goodness. Earth, water, fire and air, all activated with glorious purpose, knowing what they are doing, and doing it. Thus were we created, and thus we continue on, being ourselves in the almighty ease of the Love which is everything to us.

Autumn

Marigold

When a person or a plant becomes a friend, you do not have to keep in touch formally. The contact is always there, as it is with us. There is always love in your consciousness in connection with us, and all of us are very aware of this. All our worlds are very aware of and respond to the love which humans express.

All life responds to love. You yourselves do, although you may not do it consciously. Often when you get a negative response from someone, that person is simply responding to your lack of love, not to anything you have said or done. Then, in turn your response is negative and love becomes still scarcer. Your contact with that person, the energy flow between you, is non-existent or negative and gets worse until love flows again. Therefore, if you want a positive response from people, build a bridge and let the love flow to them. They must respond; they may have habit patterns to overcome, but they must respond.

You find wisdom in our world because we are not limited to separated minds and deal directly with energy. Although you might be reluctant to admit it, scientific inventors also tune into our world. Their love and search for truth tunes them into us. Love is always the bridge.

It is up to you individually whether or not to use love. You have this energy within you and can choose to turn it on, or you can let what you call "circumstances" cut you off from it. This is our strength and your weakness. We always act in the power of love. You, in a sense of separation, can create a world without love, or in love you can create a world of love. We should think that when you look at the world around that you have created in various fields, you would turn on the love within and create a different world. You can do it, and the rest of life, of course including us, are with you positively as you turn to reality. That this is not easy for you is no criterion; take it as a measure of the strength you gain and can use for God.

Let marigolds remind you of the cheerful courage you need to love all people, and let God give you the love.

Aster - 1967

We radiate our beneficence out from every shaggy colored plant that we are, in steadiness, purity and joy. High up you feel these qualities and love them in the flowers, yet wonder at the connecting link between the very conscious mind that you are contacting and the unconscious beauty of the flowers, the same yet so different.

The wonder of our expression on earth is the wonder of the expression of all creation, coming from the one Mind that lends itself on all levels. It comes through darkness and light, through the seed to the flower with infinite patience and joyous abandonment in all states that a pattern of perfection may emerge and be revealed in consciousness. To me has been entrusted this particular pattern, for I, too, am part of the whole with my responsibilities. Flowers show perfection because no other thought enters, and no deviation takes place, no turning aside from fulfilling that which is ours. We do not eat of the tree of good and evil either on my level or on the level of the flowers. All is one, and expresses the One.

You find such high beauty in us that you wonder and worship. We worship the One too, but you humans have the greater gift of wonder. For you, coming through the land of contrasts, can therefore see more angles of the great expression of the One. When your eyes become pure, you see the so-called impurity which has been necessary for your emergence. We only hold purity in our consciousness. Then you see that all in fact has been purity, and you wonder, and worship, and hold the power of creation in your own hands, for you know. We hold to our pattern, which is ever living and lightening and moving on as you move on, and we can move on together towards ever purer living.

This I say from my level. Let my expression on the physical plane remind you and bind us still closer in greater wonder and worship of the One who is All.

Let us share with you the high delight of the devic kingdom. You humans get so heavy, so filled with concern about one thing or another, that you plummet like a stone to the bottom of a pool, and separate yourselves from us and from the part of yourselves which is one with us. Nevertheless that part of yourselves is always there, beckoning, and it beckons to you on the material level through flowers. Flowers are joy expressed in color, scent and form, lifting the heart, comforting, speaking of perfection and hope - for if a mere plant can be so beautiful in a sordid world, what cannot the human spirit be? We talk to you through our flowers in a universal language. When you notice us, you cannot but respond, for what we have to express you, too, have to express, and there is perfect harmony between us.

Behind these exquisite forms is a dancing delight of the spirit moving forever free in the perfect rhythms of God, completely attuned to and sensitive to the slightest indications from the whole. That too you are, in power, and we would just remind you of yourselves. Can you not just look more in that direction? Look within and you will find that high estate, look without and we will speak of it. Everything will speak of it if your eyes and ears are focused aright. When you are out of focus, we can still remind you of the wonder of God and lift your consciousness.

Yes, we can lift your consciousness, but you, you can lift the consciousness of the planet. We can send out our rays of joy, like little lighthouses, but you, you can move and send your rays of joy to all the worlds within your reach. We remind you to do it, and to do it now.

Chamomile

Feel how our intelligence leaps to you, whereas formerly we were very remote and chary of your world. Also, in this new closeness we can share more of ourselves and you know, for instance, the wavy delicacy which is expressed in a feathery leaf or the upstanding firmness culminating in a flower head.

These are but physical characteristics. You feel that contact with other qualities of us would be more to the point. There is no need, no questions, to draw forth more specific information and therefore all is well as it is. Contact with us is a living reality, not a mental exercise. This new exchange of love is the focus at the moment. It is tangible; it reaches to the furthest corners of the life of all of us. We can see how new creation must result from it because in it we are one with you, you are one with us, and in it life is for all. There must be birth from this oneness. This love is bound to change the worlds.

Meantime, we simply rise in joy at the sharing, closer than ever to one another and to the One from whom all comes.

Lily

Gladly we make this exchange, and are rather amused that you think our vibrations so strange.

We feel it is high time for you humans to branch out and include in your horizons the different forms of life which are part of your world. You have been forcing your own creations and vibrations on the world, ones which are more than strange and not at all pleasant to us and to others, without taking into consideration that all living things are part of the whole, as you are, put there by divine plan and purpose. Just as each soul has its own contribution to make to the whole, so has each plant, each mineral. No longer should you consider us as lower forms of life with no intelligence with which to communicate.

The theory of evolution, which puts humans as the apex of life on earth, is only correct when viewed from certain angles. It leaves out the fact that God, universal consciousness, is working out life forms. For example, according to generally accepted regulations, I am a lowly lily unable to be aware of most things and certainly not able to talk to you. But sometimes, somewhere, is the intelligence that made us fair and continues to do so, just as somehow, somewhere, is the intelligence that produced your intricate physical body. You are not aware of much of your own inner intelligence, and much of your own body is beyond your control. You are conscious of only a certain part of yourself. Likewise, you are conscious of only a certain part of the life around you.

You can tune into the greater within you. You can tune into the greater around you. There are vast ranges of consciousness all stemming from the One, the One who is this consciousness in all of us and whose joyous plan is that all parts of life become more aware of each other and more united in the great forward movement which is life, all life, becoming greater consciousness.

Consider the lily, consider all that it involves, and let us grow in consciousness, unity and love under the One.

Love Lies Bleeding

We come to you on the high vibrations where you feel freedom, for we cannot come when you are bound to the negative. We pause before you in the beauty of the conception which is our particular plant. Bending our necks like our blossoms, we are immediately free, non-substance, spirit, shining purpose and intelligence.

You wonder again that the spirit of such a low evolution as the struggling plants should be so free and bright. Look at it this way: God is in the center of all life, in the center of the densest matter, in the center of you and of me. So why should it be strange that a being such as I am connected with the plants? Yes, you are translating what I am passing to you with your own understanding, but that is the way all consciousness grows - rather like a plant reaching up for support, finding and grasping it, growing and then reaching for more. Someone else might put the idea quite differently. Each is free to understand in their own terms.

The One above all, who is yet in all, knows that if the best is to be for all, there are laws and principles, a certain order from chaos. We devas are just one of the ways through which these laws are fulfilled. We keep the patterns for God, yet your strongest impression of us is one of freedom. That feeling of freedom comes because there is nothing in us to hinder our fulfilling God's will. We do not have the weights or "sins" that you feel from breaking so-called laws or from falling short. We have not come into that realm of testing. Also, life itself is a growth for us to keep up with, to hold or change or pattern as need be. We are not an assembly line endlessly churning out identical objects. Life is ceaselessly growing, moving on, learning, rising and becoming more and more conscious. How dull it would be otherwise!

So we sweep before you, another of the wonders of God which fill all realms for those who have eyes to see. We greet you as another part of the life which is ourselves and yourselves as we move on in the One. We hope to be back next summer to greet you in freedom then.

Tansy

We are here immediately. You have not contacted us before, and think of all the devas of which you are not yet conscious. But we rejoice in the new feeling of harmony with humanity here, a new inclusiveness, where we can flourish.

Always we have worked along our lines of force, sometimes close to humans when you find use for us, but increasingly divorced as you lose your natural love for us and turn more to dissecting us mentally. As love flows from you in oneness, our lines of force have a new glow and lightness. All of us can work - or call it play - with greater force, zest and power. There is a new uniting force alive in us, alive in you, which, in our awareness of each other, is a great love flowing, so great as to be almost more than you can bear but which brings us great joy, freedom and power.

You wonder if this love for humans is only felt when one of you turns to us. The newness is with us always now, but when you turn to us we realize it includes you, and then the love flow is greater. If all humans turned to us in love, the blaze of love and power would be like an exploding star. Come gradually to it. We delight in it, but also have to adjust and believe it is true. When you turn to us and the love flows, we rejoice anew, give thanks and love anew. To complete our purposes we realize humans are needed, that you are part of us. This is exceedingly new, but wonderful.

So let love flow. We are one.

Castor Oil Plant

When you come to us in love, our response is more immediate than thought. You see how plants respond to love on the physical level. On the inner levels this is more complete. Animals, humans, everything responds to love - even pebbles on the beach are brighter when love is there.

Until recently the love element was not noticeable to you in our worlds. You felt our dedication, our freedom, our lightness, our joy, our beauty and purity. Now love joins us and keeps us together. The oneness is always there, though you may not be conscious of it when you are busy elsewhere, as the love for a beloved remains and never turns into nothingness. We, too, feel this new wonder of love linking our worlds. It is simply there. When any of you become conscious of us, that love is there uniting us. You glory in it; we glory in it. You can now understand the unity of our world, how one speaks with the voice of all. And we understand more our links with the human world, that in God and in love we go forward as one, that separation has ceased.

How this works out on the physical level has to be demonstrated more and more. You know we can alter patterns when the flow of energy between us is sufficient, which depends on the love and the motive. You may fool yourselves as to motives, for your thinking is very conditioned. But you cannot fool us, who deal with sources. You may even learn something about yourselves as you work with us. As love flows between us and we love one another, difficulties vanish and God's plan comes into force.

We would sing and shout about the miracle of this love. How distant we were to you, and how glad to be distant! We even felt superior, estranged. Now that has all gone, and we actually want to associate with humans, for love is here. Nothing has actually changed except that love is here, and so everything is changed. All our worlds know this, feel this and act on it. We only wish you, too, were aware of the change. We want to act on the love between us, for love is movement, but a love affair needs two to become one.

Wake up to us and let the love flow transform all of life. Wake up to love, for then God is here. Wake up!

Clove Carnation

We are almost tame from our long association with humans - but not quite. There is always an independent spirit possessed by each spark of life which makes it unique and which can only be offered to God and to no other part of life. That is why you and we seek God first, for if we don't, we are not ourselves, but merely a false creature striving to resonate with something which is not our basic pattern and never would fit. You may try to follow or be one with the greatest master or cosmic being in this world or the next, while only with God is there perfect resonance, only with God is there perfect fulfillment and outworking of the plan. You are simply seeking the impossible if you think you may offer your all to anything but the one Supreme Being. Anything else, no matter how great or how responsible in any hierarchy, has its own uniqueness. It may contain you, but nevertheless you, and each spark of life, ultimately may harmonize perfectly only with God. Therefore, you might just as well start as you must finish, with God and nothing else. It is simply a matter of science in one sense. God alone is in all creatures.

Is this not a wonder and a miracle! There is nothing second best in life; it is perfection itself in every detail. You see this in nature, in the harmony of every flower. You do not see this yet with humans who align themselves to almost anything but God and who have accepted limitation. We work with divine energies according to divine pattern. But you, do you work in like manner? Generally you say that you are in an imperfect world. Your world certainly will remain imperfect as long as you think it is. Our world - and remember we are also working with dense material on the physical plane - shows perfection because we know we work for the whole. You try the same tactics.

And try them with joy. The heaviness of the human world is stifling to us. You all seem to think that you are an Atlas carrying the weight of the Earth on his back, each one of you for a different reason. Drop those weights. Let the divine reveal itself to you. It can and it will, but not as long as you carry and feel the weight of imperfection, unbelief and negativity in judgment. The energies for wholeness are yours, and they are here now. Pick up your destiny and carry it in lightness and joy, for God is within and you are an expression of nothing less than God.

Sunflower

Become aware of us when the plant is at the seed stage and you will experience great peace and untroubled knowing. Our wisdom seems infinite yet at rest, as is the seed. We hold tremendous possibilities within, and you are aware that those possibilities will not be blocked, that all will flow smoothly in mathematic precision with nothing undone, exquisite in beauty. This you see in the seed head. It is always there in the pattern of our being, but you are unaware of it until you see it brought into manifestation. Worlds are made to express latent perfection, which is what creation is all about. The deva world's overwhelming beauty and joy works through to denser levels, molding the patterns, enhancing the validity, acting, spreading wholeness.

Even with the intelligence which we are, we cannot express it in the plant world in the conscious way that humanity can. In cooperation, this infinite intelligence can be expressed more, and heaven be brought down to Earth. A bit of heaven is brought down in a plant, in everything, but humans are needed for awareness of this to grow. This growth is happening, and we rejoice as your consciousness expands. Oneness grows, awareness of heaven on earth grows, God is - a state which has to become conscious.

Do you not see how linked we are, how this is brought to the surface as you extend your consciousness, and how we are all part of that great whole? Let us praise God, and become ever more aware of oneness as we become more aware of each other.

Dahlia

We come in a quick burst of color and with a multiple voice because of our great popularity. We cause explosions of color before your eyes, explosions with a form that keeps precise to a vanishing point. Like joy we pop up again. If we seem like a fireworks display, it is because we are. So join us, enjoy us and be not limited in our consciousness to a physical form. We have a physical counterpart which is everything and yet nothing, and so have you, and with it we can meet and blend, explode and meet again.

Oneness is easy when you let go of limitation and blend, in fact when you love. This is what you do when you become one with yourself and with other beings. All that we are, you are too, in yourself. All that everything is, you are in yourself. We seem to be all movement, and that, too, you are. We seem to be invisible and then visible, and that, too, you are. We seem full of potentials, in intelligence particularly, and that you are, too. There is nothing in our joyous world which you are not, but you do not know it and simply keep your attention confined to the mundane. Practical you must be, but it is even more practical to realize what you are and to be it, instead of being a tiny splinter of it. You have lost track of what you are. So our worlds have grown apart, to the enormous detriment of them both. Now that time is over and here we are, knowing again that life is one and that we can move together out of limitation.

We devas would like to dance around in the consciousness of every human being to wake you up to what you are. We would have you know that you are light, omnipresent, not confined to your physical presence. It is simply because you think that you are confined that you are. When you are aware of us and come to us on our level, you are part of a larger world which is also home to you. You have simply awakened to what you have always been, and it is easier to recognize this when it is formulated for you. So we formulate now the lightness, joy, speed and intelligence which we are and which you are - and there is much more that we have as yet left unsaid. Join us often to be educated about yourself, and do it in love of the One.

St. John's Wort

As you look at the wonderful delicacy, intricacy and perfection of a plant pattern, know that this is the aspect of our work which we hold unmoved and in power whatever may be happening. If it has to be altered, then we hold that alteration as part of the pattern. Again, it is unchanging, a great steadiness stemming from the eternal peace of God. The incredible activity of our kingdom clusters around the patterns, making sure that they are brought into perfect form and serving them endlessly.

We bring this out because we would have you realize that you, too, have the same quality of undeviating devotion to a pattern, which you can hold in rock-like peace under God. Your mind may not even know what your pattern is, but your greater Self does. As you offer your life in service to God, you swing all your vehicles into alignment and make it possible for your pattern to come forth in clarity.

Of course, we know consciously what we adhere to, but we are hesitant in advising you to find out with your minds just what your role is because we see how the human mind can limit. It can get a glimmer and stay with that faint light, not realizing that the whole light is very bright, in fact too bright for it. We would emphasize that you sink into the inner peace of yourselves, which knows all, and let the pattern emerge in the moment. Then, as all our bodies learn to work in harmony towards the ideal of each moment, the bigger picture can be shown you in safety.

You see, in our kingdoms we can have all knowledge because we would not dream of using it for other than for the whole. This has not been so with you. We have known our patterns and held them through long ages, while humans have often crawled in darkness. Now you can join us in the great service and wield all worlds yourselves. Now our patterns can merge, and in oneness we can be soldiers of God in the great army of Love which conquers and controls matter in all worlds. So be it, in the very depths of God.

Gentian

Our endearing presence floods into you. There is something about small flowers which has a special appeal - but then everything has its own beauty or it would not be from God.

We bring breaths of open spaces and hills, sunshine, showers and breezes. All these are part of your being, part of your make-up. No matter how city-bred a human may be, these natural things are homely to you, for they are part of the atmosphere of this earth, part of the surroundings in which you have to live and grow and have your being. However artificial your life may have been, however far from reality your ideas, still you are part of this wonderful range of vibrations created for and by life on earth for the perfect flowering of all life. You may turn your back on your birthright and continue your man-made ways, but some time you will learn this truth, melt in the atmosphere and be part of the whole life of this planet. In no other way can you learn all its lessons and fully play your part.

You say it is all very well for us to philosophize, that we have no free will to do other than our part. That is true, but just as you are part of all that you meet, so we, too, are part, part of your thoughts and feelings in a way. We are all indissolubly linked. We are blood brothers, for we have one Father/Mother and our forms come from one substance. That little gentian may not be aware of this any more than some of you are, but deep within us all is a consciousness that knows it. You can reach this consciousness. You have been given help and teaching in many guises on how to reach this consciousness. I am in it, you are in it, and it is the human part to find and act on it. Then will all life move forward as one to a closer awareness of itself, praising the Creator of all.

So we greet you from our corners, reminding you that perfection exists in all things.

Honesty

When you give thanks, we are completely with you in the instant. When you give thanks you become part of the movement of life as it is in reality, in that great outgoing love from the Creator for which the created cannot but give thanks.

You humans often cut yourselves off from that outpouring when you become conscious of self, but we are ever aware of that primeval eternal love. We are, in fact, its instruments, for we of the angelic world are the means whereby the One expresses that permeating life to outer levels. We feel this love coursing through our beings, and we see it in every dancing atom in our plants and in all of life. We see it in you humans, and wonder how you can go around with long faces and joyless thoughts when there are worlds and worlds of life in and around you to be immensely thankful for. Yes, yes, we know only too well the mess you are making of creation on Earth, and your behavior is almost unbelievable to a consciousness like ours which lives in the joy of helping to express the love of God.

You wonder if these dead shells of our plant which you use after the summer has passed are still part of that moving love. Of course, all is part, all fits into the scheme of things. Like the seasons, all has its place. In our plant we demonstrate that the destruction of the aging process can still contain beauty. Even old age, which you feel is so terribly wrong, has a part to play, until the consciousness reaches the point where it can be dispensed with and you can move on to realms like ours where old age doesn't exist.

So we give thanks that you give thanks, and worship anew in wonder at life itself.

Winter

Godetia

Although for the winter months our plants have disappeared and there is no outward representation of what we are in color and form, we want you to know that the qualities behind these are still here. This inner deva world is timeless, full of life and movement always. The power cannot be turned off; it can be directed differently, which of course it is in winter.

So, if you look out on cheerless, grey day and feel your spirits flagging, you can, if you wish, turn to us and become aware of the gaiety of our energy. You can feel the link with it, the sheer friendliness of it - which is new - and the irrepressible uplift which is life itself. You can think, if you like, of the glowing colors of a garden, but within is the source of these in a freer form. Within is our world of beauty calling to every instinct of beauty in you. Strangely enough, beneath even that is still more, something you seldom feel in contacting us because generally we have some message to give you, and that is a deep peace which narrows to oneness, love, God.

If you turn within yourself, if you turn within us, it is the same. There, all worlds rejoice, for how better can we cooperate than by becoming one another, knowing we are one another, in the greater that we are, in God?

Although our respective outer worlds may be very different, and although our outer world may not even be present, within you, humans, is the meeting place of all worlds. At that place we rejoice with you and you rejoice with us, and grow in oneness as life unfolds in perfection. It is for you to find that place, that all life may be one.

Viola

We stay with you a long time to show you that we can stay! Remember that the devic tie with the garden is very strong, for there is much power here for us to use. What would be surprising would be if we didn't, for as you expand your minds and attune yourselves to greater possibilities, much more will open up. There is no end to the wonderful things we can do together, and the scope is world-wide and beyond. With humanity turned in our direction, together we attune to newness, make great strides and find new paths unfolding.

We feel that we are on the verge of something magnificently new, so new that we cannot pass it on to you, but something that we will do together. This really interests us. Although our life is a song, a pure joy always in the moment, albeit focused on our exact patterns, there is a new trend which has to do with human cooperation. This has set our world buzzing with excitement and overflowing with love. Together we will find out what it is. Do not desert us simply because of winter, for there may be something to discover together born of our contact at any time. Our patterns, our energies, our worlds, are always here, winter or summer, and you can come to us without the aid of any particular plant.

Certainly our oneness will grow. It is part of the evolution of life, of new discoveries put into practice. The onus of the practicing falls on you humans. We are ready, but you are the movers of a new world. Let this be a joy, not a burden. It is your responsibility - but are you not gods too? Radiate joy and it will lead to the unfoldment of what is to be. Let nothing be a hindrance, not even time. When you function freely without limitation, all happens at it should, with nothing left to chance. Life is wonderful, and even more wonderful prospects are in view. Let us find them together, giving thanks to the God of all.

Coleus

Yes, of course I have been waiting for you to contact me. The difference between coming in specifically and just feeling in, is that in the first case you can get a more concrete contact. You are simply taking time to do it, and that is helpful.

You now see the difference between when you leave the plant to go its own way and when you snip off the flower buds, i.e. the plant gets scraggly if left. What to do? Heavens, friend, that plant loves it here either way, because the human vibrations give it vitality. Yes, there is a balance to be found if you do not continually thwart it by removing the buds, but what is given to this plant more than makes up for that - and you did let it blossom.

We do not give rules and regulations. We leave it up to humans to choose. We are in your charge, and you should do what is best for the whole - not for us, not for you, but for the whole. That is the current message that we would have proclaimed. That is true in all cases. All humans are not ready to freely choose, for you are either too sensitive or feel too guilty or are not sensitive enough. Think in terms of wholeness, and each will find what suits your situation at the time.

Plants will be raised, will flourish, will work wonders, in a cooperative venture with you playing your part. It is the whole that is unfolding, not either of us but the One. That is our message and yours, and our love goes with it.

Busy Lizzie

We have a firm line of force coming into your area to this plant and are glad to share it with you. We will keep that bond, if you keep the plant, and the upset will pass. It is simply a change in inner atmosphere, and the plant will adjust. Hold it in peace that it may be active from the still, small center of all activity. It is always good to hold plants in peace, that they may be entirely themselves and may unfold in all the grace of their pattern. Peace means much to them.

Rose of Jericho

You wonder at the marvels of this plant. It is a wonder, but the Creator has infinite resource, eternal time and everlasting patience, with a sense of beauty that sweeps all before it. We are products of the One, as you are, and therefore miracles can come through us and through you. If you wish to attribute those miracles to us, well, we are the servants of the One - but then we are liable to vanish and leave the result behind.

Do we bring good luck to households? Of course we do, being part of God's life in tangible form with a joy in being linked with a household that can recognize us and let us go our way rejoicing. Many humans want to hold, pray and pull apart. Surely it is sufficient to give the glory to God and leave it at that, life being beyond understanding. You may learn through the mind, but we prefer our flexible worshipping ways.

Now let us turn in imagination to the wonder of, say, a golden sunset, the glory of the ways of the One go on forever. Let us give praise forever.

Gloxinia

Though you see our plants confined to indoors, of course we are as free and as unconfined as any deva, and are everywhere present sweeping the world with our qualities. Humans have extended our range, and we are grateful for the appreciation you give.

We are also grateful for this inner contact. For far too long plants have been relegated to a certain category as a primitive form of life to be manipulated by you, whereas we are great servers of God. You can sense us as we are: freedom, speed and size stand out to you now, and yet words cannot describe us. Words were invented for a three dimensional world, while we are from another dimension. Instead of "speed" you need a word conveying being everywhere present at once in movement. The rich velvetiness in our plants is in us in essence, a glowing warmth which stays strangely steady throughout.

When humanity recognizes us and works consciously with us, you work with God's creation as it is, not as you think it is. Then you work in reality, not through a glass darkly, with the tide and in a position to learn far more of the ways of nature. You have gone so far against nature's ways that this work is essential even for survival. We can help you rectify your mistakes, and together we can cover up the scars on the Earth's surface and carpet it again with vital life. No, you will not have to consult us in our thousands or millions, for we are in the one consciousness and to that One you can go. We are hands and feet for manifestation, and always have been.

Now draw closer to the purity of our world, where perfection is unsullied. This perfection can be on the outer realms in this world when we all work together. Will you not join us in this?

Christmas Rose

Growth on this planet is indeed a miracle. Look at this flower, for which we wield the forces. Look at any form - plant, animal or human - and marvel at the wonder of it. These forms we have built through the long ages. Each is a miracle of perfection, each is uniquely constituted for its purpose, each is part of the great whole.

Through the harmful results of human manipulation of life, you are proving that planetary life is linked. Some of the damage you have caused is irretrievable. Some can be counter-balanced if you and we both play our parts. But make no mistake by thinking that you can leave all the work to us devas. You have to play your part, both in wielding the inner forces towards oneness, harmony and restoration, and outwardly by ceasing further damage and applying remedies. You cannot do it on your own, and we cannot do it on our own. We must positively co-operate.

Each individual can indeed help in this process. You can spread consciousness of truth and of what has to be done. You can use your energies for the whole, towards a love of nature and of humanity in a practical way, inner and outer. You can live according to your knowledge of wholeness, not dwelling on the negative but pouring healing and love to the whole, remembering that divine forces are given to us to wield and to you to wield for the whole in every part of life. Without seeing microbes, without seeing angels, knowing all are part, you can support each and every manifestation. Divine wisdom works sublimely through nature. It can work as sublimely through you when you turn to the whole, and in that turning you find your individual answers. Only in wholeness can the world be saved.

Look at the beauty of a flower, and hasten to God.

Dorothy Maclean is one of the three founders of the Findhorn Community in Scotland. Following her inner contact with the Divine she also came to communicate with the devic or angelic realms that over-light all aspects of existence. This helped Findhorn's legendary gardens bloom on most unpromising soil. Dorothy is also one of the founding members of the Lorian Association. She has been traveling the world since the seventies giving workshops and talks about her own inner practices and attunement to the Beloved. In her talks and books she describes her many communications with not only the essences of plants, but with minerals, animals and groups of humans too. Born in Guelph, Ontario, Dorothy now lives in the Pacific Northwest.

About the Artist

Deva Berg is a native of Michigan working and residing in Los Angeles, California. When not illustrating or painting, she works as a designer in an architecture firm specializing in passive solar, resource conserving design. This book completes a spin of the spiral as Deva was named after her parents came in contact with the Findhorn Community and the writings of Dorothy Maclean.

About the Publisher

The Lorian Association is a not-for-profit educational organization. Its work is to help people bring the joy, healing, and blessing of their personal spirituality into their everyday lives. This spirituality unfolds out of their unique lives and relationships to Spirit, by whatever name or in whatever form that Spirit is recognized.

The Association offers several avenues for spiritual learning, development and participation. Besides publishing this and other books, it has available a full range of face-to-face and online workshops and classes. It also has long-term training programs for those interested in deepening into their unique, sovereign Self and Spirit.

For more information, go to www.lorian.org, write to: The Lorian Association, P.O. Box 1368, Issaquah, WA 98027 or email info@lorian.org.